Adult Literacy as Social Practice

Providing a very contemporary overview of literacy, numeracy and 'English as a Second or Other Language' teaching, this book presents a radically new perspective on reading, writing and numeracy among adults.

Since literacy is shaped by social and cultural contexts, rather than by skills and techniques alone, Uta Papen introduces a social, rather than a skills-based understanding of literacy, and discusses its relevance for adult literacy, language and numeracy education today.

Drawing on recent studies in the field of literacy and adult learning and the author's own experience as a researcher and teacher, this book shows what teachers, researchers, students and curriculum developers can gain from understanding the role of literacy in learners' lives, in relation to their families, social networks and their jobs. The books specifically offers insights into the following areas:

- how to analyse reading and writing in everyday life using the concept of a social practice view of literacy as an analytical tool;
- the role of reading and writing in everyday life, and what this tells us about learners' teaching needs;
- what is actually happening in adult basic education and how literacy is really being taught;
- how to critically examine current adult literacy, numeracy and ESOL policy in England using the tools of discourse analysis;
- how a social theory of literacy and numeracy compares with other theoretical perspectives.

With major policy initiatives coming into force, *Adult Literacy as Social Practice* will guide teachers, researchers, students and curriculum developers through this area, without the need for finding materials from different unrelated sources.

Uta Papen is Lecturer in Literacy Studies in the Department of Linguistics at Lancaster University.

New Approaches to Adult Language, Literacy and Numeracy

Series Editors: Mary Hamilton and David Barton, Lancaster University

This ground-breaking new series provides a coherent framework within which both new, and experienced, adult basic skills practitioners can develop their expertise.

Titles in this series offer key texts for adult basic skills practitioners taking professional development courses. Using a multidisciplinary approach, the theories of adult basic skills are firmly grounded in everyday practice, making the material accessible to a wide readership. The books are united by a cutting-edge approach to literacy, numeracy and ESOL, and locate this material in practical contexts, rather than purely academic debates. As well as gathering together the most important national and international research in adult literacy from the past three decades, each title also features:

- guided reading exercises
- references and further resources
- a practical research activity, linked to the topic of each book

These books are essential reading for practitioners and trainers in adult language, literacy and numeracy, covering both initial training and continuing professional development. They address curriculum and subject specifications and offer reflective and research dimensions to these topics.

Titles in the series

Adult Literacy as Social Practice: More than skills
Uta Papen

Debates in ESOL Teaching and Learning: Cultures, communities and classrooms
Kathy Pitt

Adult Literacy as Social Practice

More than skills

Uta Papen

LONDON AND NEW YORK

First published 2005 by Routledge
2 Park Square, Milton Park, Abingdon, Oxon, OX14 4RN

Simultaneously published in the USA and Canada
by Routledge
270 Madison Ave, New York, NY 10016

Routledge is an imprint of the Taylor & Francis Group

© 2005 Uta Papen

Typeset in Baskerville by Keystroke, Jacaranda Lodge, Wolverhampton
Printed and bound in Great Britain by The Cromwell Press, Trowbridge, Wiltshire

British Library Cataloguing in Publication Data
A catalogue record for this book is available from the British Library

Library of Congress Cataloging in Publication Data
A catalog record for this book has been requested

ISBN 0–415–35376–9 (Hbk)
ISBN 0–415–35377–7 (Pbk)

Contents

Series Editors' Preface

The books in this series are aimed mainly at teachers, trainers, researchers and postgraduate students concerned with the education of adults in the field of language, literacy and numeracy. They address people working and training teachers in the many contexts in which teaching and learning takes place: including colleges, family and community-based settings, workplaces and prisons. We expect the books to be useful within both initial and continuing professional development courses. They address the curriculum and subject specifications, as well as offering reflective and research dimensions for those whose interest has been sparked to probe deeper into the absorbing issues thrown up in the field. While recent national government strategies in the UK and some other countries have boosted research in the field and opportunities for professional development, as yet there are few easily available resources of the kind offered by the books in this series.

Each book in the series offers an up-to-date introduction to theory and research evidence in some aspect of the field, reviews the debates and issues and discusses how they apply to educational practice. The books are designed to be accessible to interested but non-specialist readers and each can be read independently as well as in relation to the series as a whole. The key readings and research evidence on which the books draw are international in origin and scope. Because of this and because they focus on topical debates and issues that are central to the field, the books will have wide appeal to the international research and practice community for adult literacy, language and numeracy. Development workers in a range of international contexts may also find them of interest.

These books draw on the authors' varied experience of teaching, researching and working with practitioners in short courses, summer schools, continuing professional development and networks. Each book reflects the approach of an individual author, and contains specially written discussion papers giving an overview of issues and debates, along with key readings brought together from a wide range of specialist sources. Each chapter has suggestions for exploring the material further, through reading, research activities and reflection. Key terms are explained throughout. These features, together with the access offered to key research articles in the field, make these books a unique, engaging, topic focussed resource for professional development.

As a whole, the series presents a coherent approach to literacy, numeracy and language as part of social and situated practice, seeing them as broader than simply skills to be acquired. In brief, the idea behind this approach is that literacy, numeracy and language are shaped by the social and cultural context within which they are embedded, the social relationships within which they happen, the meanings they have for users and the purposes they serve. This approach emphasises the importance of understanding the diversity of experience and knowledge that adults bring into formal learning situations and suggests ways of working in partnership with them to reflect and build on these resources in the curriculum. Over the last 15 years or so, this approach has produced some of the most exciting, leading edge thinking and research in the field and we are proud to be able to introduce this work to a wider audience and to demonstrate its relevance to policy and practice.

Adult Literacy as Social Practice: More than Skills is the first book in this new series. The main purpose of the book is to introduce readers to the key new theory about adult literacy, numeracy and language as social practice, to explain how this approach differs from conventional skills-based understandings of language, literacy and number, and to show the relevance of this approach for teachers of Adult Literacy, Language and Numeracy.

As a core book in the new series, *Adult Literacy as Social Practice* introduces both the concepts and the reflective, ethnographic methods which can be used to research adults' everyday practices. It presents an historical overview of policy and practice in the UK and offers resources to follow up on this. It includes a section on critical discourse analysis, demonstrating how this method can be used by applying it to a recent policy document.

The author, Uta Papen, has first-hand experience of literacy practice and policy in the UK, Europe and Africa. She brings her experience and insights to bear on a discussion of the comparative international dimensions of adult literacy, ensuring that this book will have a wide appeal and showing local developments in a new light.

Acknowledgements

The author and the publishers wish to thank the following for permission to use copyright material. Every effort has been made to trace all the copyright holders but, if any have been inadvertently overlooked, the publishers will be pleased to make the necessary arrangement at the first opportunity.

Chapter 1

NIACE for extracts from M. Hamilton 'Adult literacy and basic education', in R. Fieldhouse (ed.) *A History of Modern British Adult Education*, Leicester: National Institute of Adult Continuing Education, pp. 148–9
and
Language Australia (The National Language and Literacy Institute of Australia) for J. Searle (1999) *Discourses of Literacy*, pp. 7–8

Chapter 2

Routledge for extracts from D. Barton and M. Hamilton (1998) *Local Literacies*, pp. 81–5

Chapter 3

NIACE for extracts from J. Crowther, M. Hamilton and L. Tett (2001) 'Powerful literacies: an introduction', in J. Crowther, M. Hamilton and L. Tett (eds) *Powerful Literacies*, pp. 1–4

Chapter 4

Hampton Press for extracts from Judy Kalman (1999) *Writing on the Plaza*, pp. 28–33

Chapter 5

The British Association of Settlements for extracts from 'A Right to Read' (1974), pp. 4–14

Chapter 6

The Department for Education and Skills for extracts from *Skills for Life: The National Strategy for Improving Adult Literacy and Numeracy Skills, Focus on Delivery 2007* (2003), pp. 2–10

Chapter 8

Taylor & Francis for M. Hamilton (1999) 'Ethnography for classrooms: constructing a reflective curriculum for literacy', *Curriculum Inquiry*, pp. 437–9
and
RaPAL for G. Roberts and J. Prowse (1999) 'Reporting soaps', *RaPAL Bulletin* 38: 26–9

As the author, I would like to thank the various people who encouraged me to write this book and who helped me while I was working on it. My warmest thanks go to Mary Hamilton and David Barton, the editors of the series, whose enthusiasm and support for my ideas have been a great source of support since I started working in Lancaster and more specifically while I was writing this book. I would also like to thank Sue Walters, whose comments on the manuscript have provided an additional perspective to the ideas discussed with Mary and David.

I also need to thank all my colleagues at the Lancaster Literacy Research Centre: for the many cups of coffee and the chocolates that we have together, but more importantly for the friendliness, the laughter, the ideas and worries that we share and that make work at Lancaster so special.

Kay has contributed to this book in many ways and I want to thank him for all of these.

Uta Papen
Lancaster
March 2005

Abbreviations

ABE	adult basic education
ABSSU	Adult Basic Skills Strategy Unit
ALRA	Adult Literacy Resource Agency
BAS	British Association of Settlements
BSA	Basic Skills Agency
CDA	critical discourse analysis
CLA	critical language awareness
DfEE	Department for Education and Employment (now the DfES)
DfES	Department for Education and Skills
DfID	Department for International Development
ESOL	English for speakers of other languages
IALS	International Adult Literacy Survey
LEA	Local Education Authority
LLN	language, literacy and numeracy
NIACE	National Institute of Adult Continuing Education
NLS	The New Literacy Studies
NRDC	National Research and Development Centre for Adult Literacy and Numeracy
OECD	Organisation for Economic Co-operation and Development
QCA	Quality and Curriculum Authority
RaPAL	Research and Practice in Adult Literacy
SCQF	Scottish Credit and Qualifications Framework
UNDT	United Nations Development Programme
UNESCO	United Nations Educational, Scientific and Cultural Organization

Introduction

What this book is about

In September 2001, the British government launched Skills for Life, its strategy for adult language, literacy and numeracy (LLN). Although adult LLN had been a public concern ever since the 'Right to Read' campaign in the 1970s, the introduction of Skills for Life marked a new era in the provision of literacy, language and numeracy teaching for adults in England. The system, which had gradually moved from being rooted in the voluntary sector to being more institutionalised and state-funded, was completely revised and for the first time ever England now had national curricula and national standards for adult literacy, numeracy and ESOL (English for speakers of other languages).

Over the past fifteen years, along with these changes in policy, research in the field of adult language, literacy and numeracy has moved into new terrain. Conventional views on literacy (and numeracy) as abstract sets of skills have been challenged by researchers who developed a new understanding of reading and writing: not just as skills, but as social practices that are always embedded in particular cultural contexts and that are shaped by the purposes they serve and the activities they are part of. Similar ideas are being applied to numeracy and ESOL. This social practice view of literacy has provoked intense debates among academics, academics and practitioners and more recently policy-makers, not only about the nature of what literacy really is, but – more importantly – about how it is used by people in their everyday lives, how it is learned and how it can best be taught.

This book starts from a social practice view of literacy. Its primary aim is to introduce its readers to this new approach and its implications for the teaching and learning of adult LLN. The book devotes several chapters to introducing the 'theory' of literacy as social practice, but ultimately my aim is to show the readers what is the significance of this theory for the policy and practice of adult LLN, examining in particular the policy framework in England. Accordingly, the book moves from a focus on theory and research (Chapters 1–4) towards a discussion of policy and practice (Chapters 5–8). One of my key interests with this book is to show how theory and research can inform policy and practice, and vice versa. The book is strongly grounded in a reflective and participatory approach to research.

It is written in the tradition of collaboration between research and practice, an important strand of adult literacy and numeracy work in Britain.

A social view of literacy has important insights to offer to practitioners, policy-makers and researchers, complementing psychological and skills-based views on literacy. In this book, I will argue that teachers and curriculum developers have much to gain from understanding the role of literacy in learners' lives, in relation to such central aspects as their families, their social networks and their jobs. The social view of literacy is particularly suited to help us better understand:

- the role of reading and writing in everyday life and what this tells us about learners' literacy-related demands and interests;
- what exactly is going on in adult language, literacy and numeracy classrooms; how is literacy taught and learned; what literacies are being taught and how these are learned;
- current literacy, numeracy and language education policy in Britain and elsewhere.

The second aim of the book is to introduce readers to a critical approach to the study of adult literacy, numeracy and ESOL policies in Britain, using as examples policy documents and government reports from the 1970s to the present day. The major changes in the provision of adult LLN that we have seen happening in England since 2001 have provoked a lively debate amongst the general public and practitioners about the state of adult literacy and numeracy. Policies deserve critical debate. Yet teachers in particular – who often find themselves at the receiving end of policies and plans – do not necessarily have the space to reflect on their experiences and they may not feel encouraged to make their voices heard. A key aim of the book is to encourage critical reflection and constructive debate on current policies. In order to achieve this, it introduces its readers to a method of 'critical' reading of policies that draws upon the social practice model of literacy as well as on work done in the field of critical discourse analysis. While the book's primary focus is literacy, I have included numeracy and ESOL as two important strands of adult basic education, strands which have recently undergone similar major changes.

Although the book is mainly concerned with England, Scotland and Wales, the theme it addresses is important in the international arena. Researchers associated with what has become known as the 'New Literacy Studies' (NLS) have studied the literacy practices of communities in the UK, in North America, Australia and South Africa. Much research is also being carried out in other parts of the world. With regard to policy, the current changes in Britain are part of a much broader trend and many of the issues that I debate in this book, for example the question of adult literacy and numeracy being increasingly seen in terms of vocational skills, have an international dimension. Throughout the book, I draw on examples from England and other parts of the UK but also from countries as far apart as Australia and Nepal.

This book is written with two main groups of readers in mind: practitioners in adult literacy, numeracy and ESOL, and students and researchers who are interested in adult literacy, language and numeracy teaching and who are newcomers to the broad social approach to the study of literacy that the book takes.

How to use this book

The book consists of eight chapters, between this introduction and a brief conclusion. Each chapter is accompanied by a short reading (or two) that illustrates the points discussed in the main text. These readings are extracts from academic papers or policy documents. Each chapter also contains guided reading and research activities and suggested additional readings. There is also a practical research activity, linked to the topic of the book that readers can carry out alongside reading the book.

The first two chapters of the book deal with theory. Chapter 1 introduces readers to the idea of 'literacy' as a contested term, for which there is no straightforward and generally agreed definition, and suggests we think about literacy in terms of different discourses about what reading and writing are. Chapters 2 and 3 are the core chapters in which the social practice view of literacy is introduced. Chapter 2 explains the concepts of a social practice view of literacy, describes the origins of the approach and illustrates how it differs from conventional skills-based views of literacy. In Chapter 3, I deal more specifically with issues of power in relation to the role of literacy in everyday life and in educational settings. Chapter 4 is about research. More particularly, it introduces the readers to the use of ethnography as a method to study literacy as social practice.

Chapters 5, 6 and 7 focus on policy. Chapter 5 provides an overview of the history of adult literacy, numeracy and ESOL policy in England, while Chapter 6 moves on to the current policy context, concentrating on the new Skills for Life programme. Both chapters offer readers a critical perspective on policy and an introduction to the use of critical discourse analysis (CDA) for the study of policy. Chapter 7 is an example of how you can use the tools of CDA to examine in more detail the views about literacy, numeracy and ESOL that can be found in selected policy statements. The chapter serves to illustrate some of the points made already in Chapters 6 and 7; readers who are not interested in the detailed textual analysis that CDA offers may prefer to move on to Chapter 8. This final chapter discusses the practice and policy implications of a social practice view of literacy, referring in particular to current practice in England. The book ends with brief conclusions.

Useful resources and contacts

Adult Basic Skills Strategy Unit
http://www.dfes.gov.uk/readwriteplus

Adult Literacy and Numeracy Australian Research Consortium
http://www.staff.vu.edu.au/alnarc/

Basic Skills Agency
http://www.basic-skills.co.uk

Communities Scotland
(the branch of the Scottish Executive that is responsible for adult literacy)
http://www.communitiesscotland.gov.uk

Community Literacy Project Nepal
http://www.clpn.org

Lancaster Literacy Research Centre
http://www.literacy.lancs.ac.uk

National Institute of Adult Continuing Education (NIACE)
http://www.niace.org.uk

National Literacy Trust
http://www.literacytrust.org.uk

National Research and Development Centre for Adult Literacy and Numeracy
http://www.nrdc.org.uk

National Adult Literacy Agency (Ireland)
http://www.nala.ie

RaPAL (Research and Practice in Adult Literacy)
http://www.literacy.lancs.ac.uk/rapal

Some useful journals

Journal of Adolescent and Adult Literacy
Journal of Literacy Research
Journal of Research in Reading
Language and Education
Linguistics and Education
Literacies
Literacy and Numeracy Studies
RaPAL Bulletin
Studies in the Education of Adults
Ways of Knowing Journal
Written Language and Literature

Part I

A new theoretical approach

Chapter 1

Literacy – what is it?

Definitions, discourses and metaphors

What this chapter is about

In this chapter, I examine different theoretical perspectives on reading and writing and how they relate to different understandings of literacy and numeracy education. I begin by briefly examining public perceptions and media images of literacy. I then discuss different definitions of literacy that can be found in the research literature and in policy documents. My aim here is to show that these are not neutral definitions and 'literacy' is not simply a technical term, but that different concepts of reading and writing are grounded in specific discourses about literacy, about learning and about the learner. In order to explain what is meant by 'discourses about literacy', I then briefly introduce the view of language that I take in this book.

The readings that accompany this chapter provide more background to the concepts that are discussed in the main text. The discussion activities at the end of the chapter invite readers to critically examine their own assumptions about literacy and numeracy as well as on those that inform different literacy, numeracy and language programmes.

Literacy, numeracy and ESOL: the current debate

Much has been written and much is being said about what literacy is and what it means to be literate. Whether we browse recent newspapers, read the government's last election manifesto or listen to public debates on the radio, the term literacy is likely to appear. Without doubt, literacy is high on the agenda of public concerns. A quick glance at the discussion suffices to reveal the tenor of the current debate. There is much talk about changing educational demands, because of new technologies, changing workplaces and Britain's position within the global economy. There are worries that lack of literacy – or 'illiteracy' – hinders employability, leads to social exclusion and poor health, and is correlated with crime and anti-social behaviour.

We hear about falling standards and the appallingly low reading and writing abilities that many children are believed to have at the end of their school careers.

With regard to adults, recent media scares claim that low literacy standards are a major problem for the UK, with more than 20 per cent of the population believed to have 'very poor literacy skills'. These figures come from recent international studies (OECD 1995, OECD/CERI 1997, OECD 2000) by the Organisation for Economic Co-operation and Development, a powerful international body whose voice adds weight to the views of those who worry about the negative impact that Britain's poorly skilled workforce is assumed to have on the country's economic performance.

The debate easily extends to numeracy and ESOL. According to the above survey, a significant percentage of adults in England have serious difficulties with numeracy. This, together with the low levels of literacy the OECD survey reports, is believed to hamper the country's economic development and society's overall well-being. In the ongoing debate about refugees and asylum-seekers, the question of whether immigrants should be obliged to learn English is raised. Overall, this is a highly politicised debate about the future of our society and about who will be allowed to be part of it.

What emerges strongly from these debates is the high emotional and ideological value attached to literacy and the central role it plays in relation to many of our society's major concerns. Starting with the question 'What is literacy?', in the remainder of this chapter I provide an overview of different concepts of literacy and what these have to say about the literacy learner and about literacy teaching. I suggest that literacy is not a transparent concept, but a highly contested term and that we can think about it not so much in terms of definitions and common understandings, but more in terms of a 'literacy debate' (Wray, quoted in Street 1999). Rather than searching for what look like neutral definitions, we need to think about metaphors for literacy and the discourses about literacy that frame our ideas about reading and writing.

Following the Moser Report, a major review of the adult basic education (ABE) sector in England (DfEE 1999), in 2001 the British Government launched Skills for Life, a new national strategy for adult literacy, numeracy and ESOL. This development is highly relevant to those who work as practitioners in the adult basic education sector. The Skills for Life strategy is based on a set of assumptions about what literacy, numeracy and ESOL are and how best to teach them. Beginning in this chapter, I am going to examine how the assumptions about literacy that underlie particular programmes – such as Skills for Life – frame the process of teaching and learning, whether they automatically exclude other approaches and to what extent practitioners who implement the policy draw on other concepts and approaches. In doing so, I will show that different concepts had varying degrees of influence on past and present policies. In this first chapter, I invite readers to critically examine some of the concepts of literacy used by policy-makers, practitioners and researchers, and to discuss these in the light of their own experience, in the context of policies in England and elsewhere. I will begin to do this in this first chapter, but this will be an ongoing theme throughout the book.

Definitions of literacy

Among those definitions of literacy that have been around for quite a while, three concepts have been particularly influential: the functional, critical and liberal concepts of literacy.

Functional literacy

'Functional literacy' has been defined as follows:

> A person is literate when he [*sic*] has acquired the essential knowledge and skills which enable him to engage in all those activities in which literacy is required for effective functioning in his group and community, and whose attainments in reading, writing and arithmetic make it possible for him to continue to use these skills towards his own and the community's development.
>
> (Gray 1956: 24)

In the above definition, literacy is described as a skill, which is required for a broad range of activities associated with the individual's participation in society. The word 'functional' here refers not only to the society's demands on its individual members, but encompasses reading and writing that serves individual needs and purposes. In subsequent re-formulations, however, the concept became increasingly tied to economic considerations: that is, literacy became identified with the skills needed in the context of employment and economic development. At the same time, the individualistic perspective was gradually lost and, overall, the concept appeared to become more prescriptive.

Reflecting these changes, Baynham (1995: 8) notes that functional literacy is 'a powerful construct in defining literacy in terms of its social purposes, the demands made on individuals within a given society, to function within that society, to participate and to achieve their own goals'. Rassool (1999), who summarises the rise of the concept and the various changes the definition has undergone equally draws attention to the close association in most variants of functional literacy with work-related tasks, with jobs and employability, and with the demands of the economy. She suggests that the concept of functional literacy matches skills with quantifiable educational outcomes (which can be measured through adequate testing procedures) and with 'economic needs' (Rassool 1999: 6).

Central to the concept is the assumed correlation between individual skills and the overall performance of the society and the nation in terms of modernisation and economic productivity (see OECD/CERI 1997). Within this framework, functional literacy is linked to the concept of human resource development and the debate about 'basic' skills that occupies a central place in current employment policies. Literacy is seen to have high economic value and it serves as an indicator for economic and societal development.

A further term that is commonly used in discussions about literacy is the concept of 'basic literacy'. Rassool (1999: 7) defines basic literacy as 'the acquisition of technical skills involving the decoding of written texts and the writing of simple statements within the context of everyday life'. While this clearly overlaps with functional literacy, basic literacy appears to place greater importance overall on the individual and their needs, whereas functional literacy, as already argued, moves the debate away from the individual towards externally-set needs for reading and writing – that is, literacy becomes linked to work-related skills and emphasises society's demands on the individual. Both concepts, however, conceive of literacy as a set of neutral, technical skills, which have little if anything to do with culture and society. In this view, literacy in itself is valued for its assumed benefits. These are believed to be to enable learning and access to information, and thereby to support knowledge acquisition, to develop thinking and to improve the individual's chances of finding employment and income.

A functional view of literacy can be found in current definitions of adult basic education in the UK. The Moser Report for example (DfEE 1999) refers to it as '. . . the ability to read, write and speak in English, and to use mathematics at a level necessary to function at work and in society in general' (DfEE 1999: 2). However, as we will see later in this book, the functional model is not the only perspective informing ABE policy and practice in the UK.

The functional model emphasises the individual and their literacy deficits as the underlying problem. Solutions, accordingly, are to be sought by providing literacy (and numeracy) education that tackles precisely these deficits and helps people to acquire the skills they need in order to function appropriately in the workplace and in society at large (Bhola 1994, OECD 2000). In terms of educational practice, the functional model sees literacy as a fixed set of discrete skills, which are believed to be universal and transferable to all kinds of situations that require the use of written language (Barton 1994). What these skills are is of course a matter of debate, and I will come back to the question of skills repeatedly in this book.

Critical literacy

The concept of 'critical literacy' is associated with the Brazilian educator Paulo Freire, whose ideas have influenced literacy debates and literacy policies all over the world. Critical literacy refers to the potential of literacy as not only 'reading the word', but also 'reading the world' (Freire and Macedo 1987). Freire's ideas about literacy gained prominence in the 1970s and 1980s, at a time when, at the international level, faith in the functional model of literacy was beginning to fade due to the poor results many literacy programmes had produced. At this time, adult literacy work was mainly focused on the so-called developing countries, whereas industrialised nations such as the USA and the UK only slowly began to recognise adult literacy (or, as we should say, adult illiteracy) as a potential problem. I will come back to this in Chapter 5, where I describe the history of adult literacy policy in England.

Critical literacy, as Freire developed it, moves away from the 'utilitarian-vocational meanings' (Rassool 1999: 8) of the functional model, towards a pedagogy that aims to allow participants to understand their world in terms of justice and injustice, power and oppression, and so ultimately, to transform it. In this framework, literacy is conceptualised as a variable of power and it is linked to a transformative project. In other words, for Freire, literacy was political and the question of how to teach adults to read and write became part of a political project, and was no longer seen as a neutral technique as in the functional view. This opened up a whole new way of thinking about literacy programmes, what their aims are, what methods they use, what content they teach, what benefits they may bring to learners, and so on. In Freire's view, literacy involves learners' critical reflection on their social environment and the position they take within it. Freire (1972: 31–2) argued that 'what is important is that the person learning words be concomitantly engaged in a critical analysis of the social framework in which men exist'. Contrary to the functional model, critical literacy's primary purpose is not to help the individual to move up higher on the existing social ladder, but a radical critique of the dominant culture and the existing power relationships between social groups (see Shor 1993).

Freire's ideas have influenced adult educators all over the world, including in Britain (see for example Lister 1994). Hamilton (1996, see Reading 1 on pp. 17–18) refers to this critical ideology as 'literacy for emancipation' whose roots in the UK she traces back to the traditions of working-class and community education. While critical literacy need not necessarily be as radical as Freire may have thought of it, it is often linked to democratic citizenship and the role that education plays in supporting people's participation in society. This includes having the ability to not only decode the literal meanings of texts, but to read behind the lines, and to engage in a critical discussion of the positions a text supports. I will come back to this later in this book, when I will look more closely at current adult basic education policy in England and other countries of the UK.

The liberal tradition of literacy

The third concept of literacy that influences the practice and policy of literacy education in Britain is connected with the tradition of liberal adult education. In this view, literacy education is seen as a welfare activity by the middle classes for disadvantaged sectors of society (see Reading 1, pp. 17–18). The liberal tradition of adult literacy and basic education is informed by a humanist view of education that emphasises personal development and individual goals. It believes in the right to education of all citizens. Accordingly, adult basic education programmes that are informed by a liberal perspective go beyond work-related and 'functional' skills in a narrow sense, and include the more leisure-orientated uses of reading and writing, including creative writing and access to literature. Liberal adult basic education does not limit its provision to the working population, but regards literacy for older people or for those who are not part of the workforce as an equally valid activity.

Metaphors and discourses

Functional, liberal and critical concepts of literacy are not straightforward definitions, and we may not want to use the word definition at all. Rather they present us with competing ideologies of literacy, all of which use specific metaphors for literacy and are grounded in particular discourses about reading and writing. Crucially, they differ in terms of what they think the goals for literacy, numeracy and ESOL are (for the individual and for society as a whole.)

But what are metaphors for literacy and what do we mean when we talk about discourses about literacy? Barton (1994) explains how metaphors are used to describe what literacy is. A well-known example is the medical metaphor that associates lack of literacy with a disease, or a virus, which needs to be 'eradicated'. Note that many of these metaphors, although speaking about literacy, in reality refer to illiteracy. We have all heard about the 'literacy crisis', which in fact is referring to illiteracy! Metaphors for literacy do not stand on their own. They are part of a particular view on literacy that has implications for how we think about learners, how we think about what they ought to learn and how this could be achieved. Metaphors for literacy are part of broader clusters of meaning; they are part of discourses.

What is a discourse?

Discourses can be described as themes, attitudes and values – expressed through written and oral statements, images and behaviour – which at a given time and place, within a certain institutional or non-institutional context are deemed meaningful (adapted from Gee 1999: 37). Crucially, discourses not only claim to be meaningful, but they also make a claim to truth.

The notion of discourse, however, is not straightforward, and there are different understandings of what it means. In linguistics, the term discourse is often used to talk about extended stretches of text (in the broad sense, referring to both oral and written language). Discourse, in this sense, refers to the forms of language associated with specific registers and genres. Examples would be the discourse of a job interview compared to the discourse of friends at a dinner party. These are different registers. With regard to written language, we use the term 'discourse' when we talk about the particular lexical and grammatical forms of texts types or genres, such as novels or business letters. Such genres are conventionalised, and this means that we recognise social rules and conventions for writing in particular ways when addressing different people.

It is helpful to distinguish between 'discourse' as an abstract noun and 'discourses' as a count noun. As an abstract noun, discourse is used in the way I explained it above. As a count noun, discourses represent or describe particular aspects of the physical, social and psychological world (see also Fairclough 2003: 26). This latter understanding of discourse is the one I use in this book. Crucially, this goes beyond the linguistic understanding of the term.

Discourses – with their themes, attitudes and values – are grounded in an understanding of language as mediating our knowledge and understanding of the world. What I mean by this is that language is not a transparent tool to represent reality, but is in itself involved in the construction of reality. We use language in order to make sense of the world, to make sense of what happens to us. We also use language in order to communicate our understanding of the world to others. But language is not conceivable as separate from thinking and acting and, as we all know too well, we think while we talk and we are not always conscious of the thoughts that initiate and guide our actions (and at times we wished we had done the thinking before we did the talking or the acting). What I am trying to suggest here is twofold. Firstly, language – and this is precisely what discourse in the more sociological or philosophical sense that I use it means – is not neutral: it is part and parcel of how we structure knowledge and how we construct relationships between people. Secondly, the language we use (and this applies to all instances of language use, including written and oral language) is to some extent given and socially controlled.

A way to think about discourses is to see them as sets of statements, which together form a consistent position about something. Discourses give expression to an opinion, for example about literacy, and this opinion is based on shared beliefs, assumptions and values. However, it would be wrong to think of these beliefs as 'having been there already'. To some extent, discourses of course represent ideas that are already there. However, discourses in themselves are part and parcel of the construction of particular views and they are an important medium through which certain positions are being spread and enter different people's views and beliefs. Most importantly, discourses are about who has the power to raise an opinion and who is in a position to influence how others form their views.

Discourses are 'about what can be said and thought, but also about who can speak, when, where and with what authority' (Ball 1990: 21). Without doubt, there were things that could be said and were being said about literacy in Britain in the year 2004. Frequently, there was talk about low levels of literacy as a drain on the economy. Illiteracy, it was said, hinders those who cannot read and write from finding jobs and from performing all those tasks that are essential to their participation in society. The linking of literacy to social exclusion was a recent view that had emerged as part of the government's new commitment to adult language, literacy and numeracy. Other statements, however, were made less frequently and some could not be made at all. We rarely, if ever, heard anybody questioning the value of literacy and the need for everybody to be able to read and write. Talking about literacy, we have an idea about who is in a position to speak, and whose voices are much less likely to be heard. Much too often, these unheard voices are the voices of practitioners and of the learners themselves.

Normalisation

Discourses tell us something fundamental then about how in society we come to believe what we deem to be facts and what we accept as shared knowledge.

Foucault (1980) called this a process of 'normalisation': the acceptance of statements as norms, as being obviously and inherently 'true'. Such discourses are often tied up with powerful institutions, for example schools or further education colleges that support a particular view on literacy. Through the authority of the education system, standards of literacy are set and ways to achieve these standards are determined. Yet, while many of us rarely question the powerful discourses of such public institutions and the media, we nevertheless have our own discourses and these may or may not correspond with the dominant views about reading and writing.

It is important to see that discourses are not only about language or about what can be said. Crucially, discourses influence and shape practice: they establish what are accepted as appropriate and legitimate ways of action. The way that a problem is defined determines what are believed to be its causes and what action can be taken to address it. Discourses then are about what policies will be developed, what kinds of literacy programmes will be offered, what curricula will be written and what assessment tools will be designed.

Why then should we think in terms of discourses rather than definitions of literacy? The notion of discourse allows us to address three inter-related questions. Firstly, it allows us to see that what appears to be a neutral definition of literacy is in fact part of a much broader ideology, or, to use the new term, part of a discourse about literacy. This discourse, for example the discourse of functional literacy, makes a set of assumptions about the reasons for lack of literacy, the value of attaining literacy and the impact of enhanced literacy on the individual and on society. Definitions about what literacy is are always situated in such discourses.

Secondly, if we think about normalisation in the sense of some people or some institutions trying to impose their way of looking at literacy on others, we can begin to look at power in relation to literacy. We can ask who determines what literacy levels people need to attain, what kind of reading and writing skills they should acquire and how this should be achieved. And, whose interests are being served by a particular literacy policy?

Thirdly, discourses make statements about people. They are closely connected with identity. To be more concrete, discourses refer to how people's identities are socially constructed and how we, as we identify with common cultural values and norms of behaviour, experience ourselves in terms of discursive categories. Many of those who do have problems with reading and writing might not necessarily think of themselves as the 'functionally illiterate' that the media often speak about. They may not think about themselves as lacking basic skills. However, the current policy discourse of literacy in Britain declares some people as literate, and others as illiterate. Equally, it declares some as being numerate, and others as having serious problems with numeracy.

The Skills for Life strategy (which I discuss in detail in chapters 6 and 7) identifies a number of groups as 'target' populations for the new policy. It requires those who are unemployed and receive benefits to participate in mandatory literacy and numeracy 'screening', forcing them to make public their assumed difficulties with reading, writing and calculating. The currently dominant discourse about literacy (and numeracy, which is often subsumed under the term literacy) has a particular view of those who are presumed to lack literacy. It makes assumptions about the links between lack of literacy and unemployment, poverty, social exclusion, poor health and anti-social behaviour. Thinking in terms of literacy as a discourse invites us to look at how people are being positioned by dominant discourses and how terms like literacy, illiteracy, functional literacy and others categorise people and impose social identities (Gee 1996).

The notion of discourses then helps us to look behind the apparently obvious statements we find in policy documents, mission statements and research reports. In later chapters of this book, I examine such documents and try to deconstruct the 'preconstructed' notions of literacy that inform the policy and practice of literacy education. I also raise questions that challenge common assumptions about literacy. Is literacy the common good that nobody in today's society can live without? Does improved literacy really lead to better employability? And what about the people who come to literacy, numeracy or ESOL classes in order to get support with their literacy and numeracy-related problems? How do they think about literacy and what do they believe they can gain from it? Do they agree that lack of literacy and numeracy is one of their fundamental problems? And what about those people whom the policy claims to target, but who never come?

Policy papers are important to look at. But discourses, such as the discourse of literacy as a skill, are not located only at the level of policy. They permeate all levels of a literacy programme, because they are articulated through the curriculum, through textbooks and through suggested teaching and assessment practices. Accordingly, it is important to examine how these discourses are reflected in curricula and textbooks, and what influence they have on the actual process of teaching and learning. In the course of this book, you will take a critical look at some policy documents and at extracts from the new national curricula.

What does all this mean for adult language, literacy and numeracy practitioners?

We have seen that there is no single definition for what literacy is. More importantly, we have seen that it is perhaps not possible, perhaps not even desirable, to have such a common definition. Definitions, as I have argued, are not neutral, but are part of discourses, which in turn make assumptions, set values and try to impose standards.

The above discourses have important implications for the practice of adult literacy, numeracy and ESOL. Practitioners – by which I mean anyone who works face-to-face with students in LLN, or who is involved in designing or running an LLN curriculum or programme – draw on these positions to inform their own teaching. While all three approaches – functional, liberal and critical – inform adult language, literacy and numeracy policy and practice in the UK, nonetheless since the late 1980s literacy has moved closer to vocational education. As a result, a discourse of literacy as technical skill and vocational competence has become dominant. This trend is not at all unique to Britain. Searle (1999: 13) commenting on recent policy development in Australia, writes that the country has witnessed the 'mainstreaming of literacy in vocational education'. As its title already indicates, the new Skills for Life strategy thinks of literacy and numeracy primarily as skills. I have shown earlier in this chapter that in public debates about adult literacy the notion of skills occupies a central position. It seems fair to say, then, that the skills view of literacy is the dominant position that shapes current adult LLN policy. But if this is the case, we need to ask (and we will do so in the coming chapters) what forms of adult LLN provision are developed based on this dominant model. How successful is the current model? Whom does it reach, who benefits from it and who is left aside?

A further question is whether those who work in the field of adult language, literacy and numeracy agree with this view. Is literacy mainly about reading and writing as vocational skills? Is adult LLN's main, and perhaps only, task to prepare adults with reading and writing difficulties to master the kind of skills they need for employment? And what happens to the principles of humanist and emancipatory adult education, if literacy becomes increasingly subsumed under a discourse of human resource development and economic productivity? The question for prac-titioners may be: 'How to stay true to adult literacy principles while working within the technicist discourses?' (Searle 1999: 13).

These are important questions to ask and I come back to them in later chapters of this book. Another key issue is whether literacy is best understood as a set of skills, which – once they have been acquired – can be applied independent of the context of use. Most people would probably agree that in some sense reading and writing are skills. But does the term 'skills' cover everything there is to literacy and numeracy? Does it really tell us what literacy is? Or, is it too simple to say that literacy is a set of skills, one that everyone ought to possess? We need to ask if there is no other way of describing literacy than thinking of it in terms of coding and decoding skills.

From your own experience you will know that literacy is not necessarily the same for everyone. There are different ways of using literacy, or – as we might want to say – there are different forms of literacy. Could it be useful to think and talk about literacies in the plural, not literacy? In the next chapter, I introduce a new way of thinking about literacy, which looks at reading and writing not as single skills or a single set of competencies, but as a whole variety of social practices.

📖 Readings

The two short readings for this chapter discuss various discourses about literacy. Hamilton distinguishes between three such discourses (which she calls ideologies). Searle in her paper lists a number of discourses, including 'literacy as autonomy: basic skills', 'literacy as a right: social justice', 'literacy for social action: transformation' and 'literacy as technology'. The extract from her paper that is printed below talks about 'literacy as control'. When you have read both texts, you can try the tasks below.

Reading 1:

Hamilton, M. (1996) 'Adult literacy and basic education' in R. Fieldhouse (ed.) *A History of Modern British Adult Education*, Leicester: National Institute of Adult Continuing Education, pp. 148–9.

Literacy for emancipation implies a radical critique of elite culture, selective schooling, state or religiously controlled curricula and existing unequal power relations among different social groups. This is a continuation of the oppositional traditions of independent working-class education described in Chapters 8–10, where adult education is linked to political organisation and action and serves the interests and purposes of working people (Simon, 1992). It is also part of the tradition of community education, where education is linked with efforts to change power structures in order to increase the resources available to communities (see Chapter 5).

Within this discourse, ABE addresses issues of power and representation by emphasising the need for social and political change to redress language-based inequalities. Issues of access to reading and writing are seen as issues of power, not just technical issues of language. Whilst this strand resonates strongly with the Freirian approach to literacy (Freire, 1972) it would be a mistake to think that Freire's ideas were a widespread inspiration for ABE work in this country. Those who were aware of his ideas *did* try to make the connection with their own work, and also with the other mass literacy campaigns that have taken place as part of revolutionary social change this century (Brown, 1973; Arnove and Graff, 1987). The challenge for the new ABE was to adapt Freire's analysis to a society where in principle everyone has access to basic education through primary schooling (Kirkwood and Kirkwood, 1989). A critique of the existing system of schooling was therefore needed.

In the competing discourse of **literacy for social control** by dominant groups, literacy is seen as a way of maintaining the status quo, functionally shaping responsible, moral and economically productive citizens. It may be seen in its purest forms in relation to employer-led workplace training or in prison education, but elements of the social control discourse also occur in the most prominent ideological strand in British ABE whereby literacy education is seen as a welfare activity promoted by the middle classes for disadvantaged 'others' as a way of offering enlightenment – opening access to literacy, classical or religious culture – a kind of **cultural missionary activity**. Whilst this discourse is almost entirely secular in its expression in contemporary society, we have already noted the very overt social and moral control of literacy that sprang from religious motives in earlier days, and which has left a powerful legacy (Graff, 1987).

Discourses of social control within ABE make frequent appeals to liberal and democratic arguments, but in practice the definition of culture on which they are based has generally been extremely narrow – ridden with class-based hierarchical notions of 'good' and 'bad' language, high and low culture. It has also been shaped by imperial notions of the superiority of the English language as a symbol of nationhood, leading to racist, deficit notions of bilingual speakers and a total neglect of serious policy to address the needs of linguistic and cultural minorities. Such attitudes, of course, pervade language policy and practice across the whole educational system and ABE has had to work within the constraints posed by these (Carby, 1982; Brumfit, 1985). An important issue in evaluating the contribution of ABE is, then, how far it has managed to resist and critique this discourse.

Another legacy from the general educational discourse as described above has been the **deficit model of literacy** carried over to ABE from remedial or special needs education and, more broadly, from the selective educational tradition. How could ABE and ABE students define themselves in ways other than this remedial discourse and develop positive views of those adults who do have learning difficulties?

One way is to move away from an individual, skills-based approach to ABE towards a view of literacy and numeracy as community resources to which ABE can improve access for individuals and groups.

These four strands (emancipatory, social control, cultural missionary work and remedial views of ABE) have been tightly interwoven in the fabric of ABE in the UK. Most programmes show evidence of a mixture of them and any analysis must focus on the shifting balance of power between these different ideologies at different points in time, or in different institutional and policy settings.

Nevertheless, they are useful pointers for evaluating the changing shape of ABE as it moved from the early days of the literacy campaign and for identifying the areas in which a truly effective ABE would have to develop a critical stance. These are: (1) a critical analysis of the social and economic relationships framing literacy in the UK, especially in respect of the world of work; (2) a cultural critique exposing and contesting the elitest assumptions in discourses about language and literacy; and (3) a critique of the formal educational system, especially the ways in which it creates deficit models of literacy learners.

Reading 2:

Searle, J. (1999) 'Literacy as control' in *Discourses of Literacy*, Queensland: Language Australia, pp. 7–8.

An historical overview of literacy, such as that presented in Appendix 2, shows that as a concept 'literacy' has never been politically neutral. In many societies, literacy has been used as a means of maintaining power and control, whether by religious, government, bureaucratic or trading groups with vested interests. The ancient Greeks for example, perfected the use of rhetoric as a means of persuasion or social control. Writing was denounced as encouraging mental laziness (Ong, 1982) and also because it could be interpreted by the reader in many ways other than those intended by the author. This powerful argument was subsequently presented as a rationale for restricting access to literacy as a means of religious control. For example, literacy in the Catholic tradition was reserved for church authorities only, for fear of incorrect interpretations (Heath, 1986; Gee, 1990). In contrast, the Swedish literacy campaign of the 17th century advocated the teaching of reading, of horn (prayer) books, in order that people might read God's word with their own eyes. Nevertheless, such 'reading' was strictly mediated by religious authorities (Arnove & Graff, 1987; Graff, 1986). This tradition is continued today through a range of fundamentalist religions in which a literal 'reading' is required.

As a result, literacy became gendered and elitist, that is, restricted to two classes of men, the upper classes of society (priests, rulers, scholars and the military) and the middle-class traders. Such users of literacy reflected the various power relations (civic, religious and military) within society (Gough, 1988). In addition, alongside the use of literacy for commercial purposes was the need for written records for administrative and bureaucratic purposes, traditions which continue today, some of which are documented in Appendix 2.

With the industrialisation of Western Europe came mass education. Whereas previously, an elite form of education based on a classical tradition had been available to the upper classes, now, all children were required to attend compulsory schooling. However, the purpose of public education at this time was again as a form of social control, to produce sober, law abiding citizens (Limage, 1987) and compliant workers. As a result, public education was limited to rote learning, drill and copying in a fair hand (Donald, cited in Green, 1993). Importantly, the policy of using education as part of a civilising process was one which also extended to the colonies, particularly in relation to the indigenous populations, though with varying degrees of 'success' (see Fesl, 1993).

Similar views on the importance of education would also have informed UNECSO, an organisation which, since the end of World War II, has been at pains to quantify, explain and remedy the problem of 'illiteracy'. Although the focus has been on measuring the extent of adult 'illiteracy' by gathering statistics on access to schooling, in developed, developing and underdeveloped countries, it could be argued that these campaigns represented another aspect of social control. Initially seen as 'developmental', the early UNESCO literacy campaigns and the World Bank literacy programs were based on the premise that a literate population would somehow increase the productivity and hence the economic development of their country. The mass literacy campaigns, particularly in the developing Third World, focused on 'inoculating' individuals with literacy in order to achieve cognitive enhancement, social and economic development. They also had a political agenda, being "something of a crusade . . . the moral equivalent of war" (Bhola, 1982 cited in Arnove & Graff, 1987: 3). But as Limage (1993: 23) stated, "When learners in these . . . programs discovered that the only 'functionality' involved was to make them better workers, the majority of the experiments failed". Limage and others questioned not only the actual purpose of the campaigns, but also who had (or has) access to literacy (in relation to gender and class).

Research

1   Collect as many definitions of literacy as you can (from policy documents, websites and the research literature). How would you describe these definitions? What assumptions about literacy, about learning and the learner do they make? Use Hamilton's three ideologies to help you with this. Compare these definitions with your own understanding of literacy.
2   Collect statements about literacy found in newspapers and magazines. What metaphors for literacy do they use? To what discourses about literacy do these metaphors belong?

Reflection

Think of a literacy/ numeracy/ ESOL programme you know well – or try to imagine how one might be run. Does it fit in one of Hamilton's categories? Explain why.

Additional reading

Barton, D. (1994) *Literacy – An Introduction to the Ecology of Written Language*, Oxford: Blackwell, Chapter 2.

Verhoeven, L. (1994) 'Modeling and promoting functional literacy', in L. Verhoeven (ed.) *Functional Literacy. Theoretical Issues and Educational Implications*, Amsterdam: John Benjamins, pp. 3–35.

Chapter 2

A new way of looking at reading and writing

Literacy as a social and situated practice

What this chapter is about

At the end of Chapter 1, I suggested that to view literacy (and numeracy) merely as a skill misses out important aspects of what is happening when people read and write. In this chapter, I pursue this argument and present an alternative to the common view of literacy as just a skill: the idea of literacy as a social practice. I will explain what the concept of literacy as social practice means and how it was developed, mention some of the researchers who favour it and briefly describe examples of studies that are associated with what are called the 'New Literacy Studies'.

In order to introduce the main concepts of the social practice view of literacy, I am going to discuss a particular set of literacy-related activities: the reading and writing that takes place when buying tickets and travelling by train. Using the train as an example, I will also discuss the idea of numeracy as a social practice, numeracy being often integrated with literacy.

In Chapter 3, I continue this discussion by looking more closely at the roles of institutions and relationships – and their power – in shaping particular literacy practices. This will provide ample opportunity to discuss the role of power in relation to literacy practices. Throughout both chapters, my main aim is to familiarise readers with the ideas and concepts of a social practices view of literacy. At the same time, I will begin to raise the question that will be at the centre of the remaining chapters of this book: what are the implications of a social practices view of literacy for the policy and practice of adult literacy, numeracy and ESOL provision?

Literacy debates: skills versus practices

In the previous chapter, I introduced three concepts of literacy: functional, liberal and critical literacy. These three approaches differ in how they define the content and purpose of adult literacy. While they all agree that reading and writing are things people need to learn how to do, they disagree on how this can best be achieved. They also diverge on how they describe the activities of reading and writing. There are indeed ongoing debates among educators, researchers and the general public as to the nature of reading and writing. The 'reading wars' are witness of such intense and at times heated discussions. Much of this refers to schools and to what are deemed to be the best ways of teaching children how to read and write, although the issues are similar when referring to adult literacy. In recent years, researchers have contributed to these debates by adding a fourth way of thinking about literacy, and it is to this relatively new concept that I turn now.

You may have noticed that in the previous paragraphs I referred to the 'activities' of reading and writing. I could have used the word skills instead of activities. My choice of words was of course not innocent. Whether we think of reading and writing primarily as skills, that is, the ability to code and decode letters and words, or as activities, meaning things we do with letters and words, shifts the emphasis onto different aspects of what literacy means. In fact, it does much more than shift the emphasis. Talking about skills – or not – means touching upon a central question in the debate over literacy. Is literacy a cognitive or a thinking skill? Is it a technique? Is it an emancipatory act (as the discourse of critical literacy suggests)? Or should it be seen as a social practice? I have already said in the previous chapter that the functional discourse thinks of reading and writing primarily as a set of autonomous skills or techniques, which can be applied to different contexts of use. We can call this the 'skills view' of literacy.

The skills view is associated with a psychological and cognitive understanding of literacy that looks at it from the point of view of individual ability. Many educationists see themselves as part of this side. Those who see literacy as a universal set of coding and decoding skills have traditionally had a particularly strong position within the field of adult LLN policy and practice. In terms of teaching, this side argues in favour of a code-based approach, and instruction that focuses on the phoneme/grapheme (sound/letter) relationship. Those who adhere to a skills view of literacy would support the need for schools and adult literacy classes to concentrate much of their work on the teaching of phonics.

Meanings of literacy that are associated with the skills view

The skills view is common among the general public. It typically associates literacy with certain forms of reading and writing, and certain text types or genres, and in most cases these are the texts and activities we are familiar with from school – for example, story books, grammar and spelling exercises, or dictations. The skills view links literacy to education and erudition, and the ability to read and write is often regarded as a first and necessary step for people to become 'educated'. The skills view of literacy is close to what Barton (1994) calls a 'literary view' of literacy and again this is strong in many people's ideas about literacy. In a study conducted in the USA, Bialostok (2002) asked 15 middle-class parents of kindergarten children about their understanding of literacy. His aim was to get behind these parents' taken-for-granted views of literacy. His discoveries of the 'cultural models of literacy' (Bialostok 2002: 349) held by these parents reveal that many of them associated literacy with morality, with connotations of good and bad people. Parents were talking of literacy in relation to purity and they expressed the belief that literacy supports empathy with other people. They also described literacy as something that was simply part of their personality. In this sense, literacy was seen less as a skill than as a personal attribute.

Many of the interviewed parents also linked literacy (as the ability to read) to power and economic well-being, and they referred to the forms of knowledge and understanding the able reader has access to. While it is difficult to refute such a view, it is important to see the narrow understanding of knowledge that it rests upon. It supports the idea of knowledge as that which can be found in books (or, increasingly, on websites) and disregards and devalues oral knowledge and life experience. The same view more or less automatically presumes that someone who is educated is necessarily literate. I will come back to these ideas a little later in this chapter.

Bialostok's study revealed important insights as to what the interviewed parents had in mind when they talked about the meaning of literacy in their lives. When talking about activities that involved literacy, all the interviewed parents referred to book reading. None of them talked about reading the label on a milk bottle or finding a telephone number in a phone book. For them, this kind of reading was not part of their construct of literacy. And yet, and this is the point I will expand on now, reading the print on a bumper sticker, on a shirt or a sign, is also literacy. The same is true for writing. Writing a novel is literacy. But so is filling out a tax form or sending a text message to a friend.

Challenges to the skills view

In recent years, the skills view has been challenged for its inability to capture either the variety of literacy-related activities that individuals and communities engage with in their everyday lives or the range of meanings literacy has, depending on its social and cultural context of use. Because of its narrow conception of what counts as reading and writing, the skills model ignores many of these activities. Those who believe literacy to be not just a skill, but a social and cultural practice, emphasise the multiple forms of literacy that are part of our everyday lives and the multiple ways in which all of us – so-called illiterate and literate people – engage with written texts. They challenge the skills view, and the functional literacy programmes based on its premises, for its lack of success in helping adults with the reading and writing tasks that occur in everyday life, at work and in the home.

Critics of the skills model also point out its inability to explain the processes of informal learning through which we learn to deal with unfamiliar types of texts, learn to adapt our style of writing to the requirements of new technologies or learn to navigate the literacy environment of unfamiliar institutional settings (cf. Tusting and Barton, forthcoming). How do you find your way around a hospital you have never been to before? Do you remember how you first learned to use a computer? Have you ever watched young people texting at incredible speed and asked yourself how they learned to do so?

In the rest of this chapter, I take a closer look at the idea of literacy as a social practice (Street 1993, Barton 1994, Gee 1996, Barton and Hamilton 1998). This view looks at reading and writing not only as skills, but as social activities that are always situated in particular cultural and historical contexts (Barton, Hamilton and Ivanič 2000).

Literacy as social practice

What does it mean to say that literacy is a social practice? Why is literacy social? What do people mean when they refer to literacy as a practice?

In order to understand what a theory of literacy as social practice means, it is best to compare it with the skills view. I have already said that this view regards literacy as a set of skills, which are independent of their particular context of use. The social practices view of literacy (which is also referred to more simply as the 'social view of literacy') believes that things are not as simple as that. Advocates of the social view believe that we have to look at literacy not merely as a skill, as something people have learned and therefore know, but as something people do. This means we should think of literacy not so much as an 'attribute' (usually believed to be vested in the individual) but as an activity (Tusting and Barton forthcoming). People read and write in order to achieve specific purposes. What they do with literacy is part of a broader activity they engage in. It is these activities that give meaning to people's reading and writing. Accordingly, if we want to understand what literacy is about, we need to look at the social activities of which literacy is a part (Barton and Hamilton 2000).

A central pillar of the social practices view of literacy is the idea that there are many different forms of literacy – or many literacies, as we can say. The examples I referred to in the previous section give an idea of this variety. Reading a book is not quite the same as reading the 'best before' date on a milk carton. Writing a text message is different from writing an essay. Thinking about technologies, there are many other forms of literacy, such as reading a web page. As the reader of a web page, you have to make continuous choices about your 'reading path', whereas in a printed book the pathway through the plot is given. The question thus is how different are these two literacies and do they really support the idea of a plurality of literacy practices? From a skills perspective, you may still want to argue that although these are different ways of using script, they all rely on the same underlying ability: coding and decoding. The additional abilities required are variants of this basic skill.

A social practices view of literacy would counteract this argument by highlighting not only the variety of skills needed for various literacy practices, but by drawing attention to the different meanings and purposes these literate activities have, depending on what technologies they involve, who uses them, in what context and for what ends. Variety in language use seems to be much more widely accepted when talking about spoken language (Barton 1994). We are all familiar with the idea of different dialects, accents and registers. Written language generally is believed to be more stable. Yet, if we think about the above examples, this is perhaps not quite true. There is great variety in written language. Once we accept this view, the idea of different literacies becomes less alien.

We can see from the above that part of what makes literacies distinct from each other is their use for different purposes and the way they are embedded in particular contexts and activities. This is an important thrust of the social practices view of literacy: literacy practices are always embedded in a social and cultural context. But what does this context consist of? Obviously, this depends on the particular reading and writing activity. Accordingly, any researcher who examines people's reading and writing practices needs to take a close look at this context, and describe it in as much detail as possible. This calls for the use of ethnography, a particular form of qualitative research, in the study of literacy. I discuss ethnography and its use for the study of literacy in detail in Chapter 4.

Suffice to say here that ethnography refers to close, in-depth examinations of social activities as they naturally occur in real-life settings. There are certain elements to look out for when studying literacy from an ethnographic perspective (adapted from Hamilton 2000):

- There are always people involved in a literacy event. The term 'literacy event' here refers to any social activity in which reading and writing, or texts, play an essential role. Shirley Brice Heath (1983: 50) defines a literacy event as 'any occasion in which a piece of writing is integral to the nature of the participant's interaction and their interpretative process'.
- Something is happening in a literacy event, there is some activity: the actions of those who take part in the literacy event.
- There is always a written text involved and much of the activity going on will focus on this text. But there will also be a lot of talk and interaction, and some of this is likely to be 'talk around text'.
- This literacy activity is embedded in a social and institutional context. The context includes the immediate setting in which the literacy event takes place, and the domain of social and cultural practice to which it relates (such as school, workplace or community).

An example: train literacies

Consider, for example, the activity of someone in Leeds taking a train in order to visit their mother who lives in London. There is quite a lot of reading and writing involved when travelling by train. First of all you will have to buy a ticket. Let's assume that you do not know the train times for London and that you will want to buy your ticket in advance. You can do this either by going to the station or by phoning the train company. Alternatively, you might buy your ticket through the train company's website. On the website, you can find out about train times and enquire about the most direct route and the cheapest fares. Instead of logging onto the company's website, you can use National Rail's online timetable to check train times and connections.

In whatever way you proceed, you will need to do quite a lot of reading and writing. You will also have to do some calculating, when deciding between different train times and different fares. Is it worth buying an open ticket? How much more expensive than the 'apex' ticket would that be? What is the likelihood of my having to change my departure time? These are some of the questions you will consider.

The important thing about all the reading, writing and calculating going on when buying a train ticket is that it is done as part of a broader social practice, which in this case we might want to call 'travelling by train'. In the above example, literacy and numeracy are embedded in the social practice of using trains. A further crucial point is that you cannot understand what reading and writing in this context are about without knowing something about how trains in Britain operate. You need to be familiar with the social rules and conventions of transport in this country. Without this knowledge, you cannot understand why travellers read particular things, such as the timetables or the numbers of the coaches, but not others (they don't necessarily read the train company's magazine that they find on their seat).

To give you an example, visitors from another European country, let's say from Germany, whose rail transport system has not been privatised, will at first not understand why it is important for travellers in Britain to know with which train company they travel. The first time the visitors buy a ticket, they may not know what an 'apex' ticket is and what the difference is between the 'saver return' and the 'standard plus' fare. Although most of this information is given somewhere on the website or in the company's brochure, even the 'cultural insider' who grew up in Britain, might not be aware of all the conditions that apply to the different fares.

Numeracy is an important part of the social practice of travelling by train. It is crucial when calculating prices for rail tickets, when checking train times and even more in case your train is late and you wonder whether you will still be able to get your connection. Many people simply go to the train station or to a travel agent when having to find out about a complicated journey that involves several changes. In this case, the travel agent will do the more difficult jobs for you: finding out about train times on National Rail's website, checking fares in the different train companies' price lists, and so on. She serves as a 'literacy mediator', an idea to which I will come back in Chapter 3. However, instead of seeing an agent, you may search for the relevant information yourself. Have a look at Figure 2.1. This is an example of an itinerary for a cross-country journey found on the National Rail 'Planning your journey' website.

The page is a particularly telling example of the integration of literacy and numeracy that is common in many everyday texts. In order to know when to take which train, you need to understand letters and numbers. One of the most important aspects of this journey plan is being able to calculate the time available

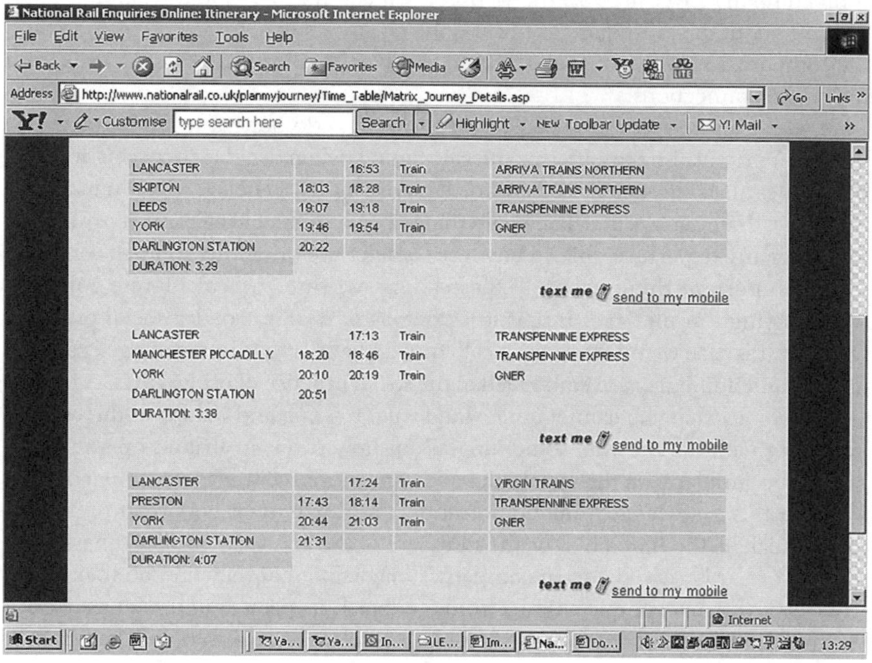

LANCASTER		16:53	Train	ARRIVA TRAINS NORTHERN
SKIPTON	18:03	18:28	Train	ARRIVA TRAINS NORTHERN
LEEDS	19:07	19:18	Train	TRANSPENNINE EXPRESS
YORK	19:46	19:54	Train	GNER
DARLINGTON STATION	20:22			
DURATION: 3:29				
LANCASTER		17:13	Train	TRANSPENNINE EXPRESS
MANCHESTER PICCADILLY	18:20	18:46	Train	TRANSPENNINE EXPRESS
YORK	20:10	20:19	Train	GNER
DARLINGTON STATION	20:51			
DURATION: 3:38				
LANCASTER		17:24	Train	VIRGIN TRAINS
PRESTON	17:43	18:14	Train	TRANSPENNINE EXPRESS
YORK	20:44	21:03	Train	GNER
DARLINGTON STATION	21:31			
DURATION: 4:07				

Figure 2.1 National Rail Enquiries Online Itinerary

for changes in Manchester, Leeds and York. How many minutes do I have to change trains in Leeds? What happens if the Manchester train is ten minutes late? Will I still be able to catch my train to York? These are just some of the questions travellers are likely to ask themselves. Things become even more complicated if you do not know the train stations where you have to change. Whether four minutes are enough to change from the Manchester to the York train at Leeds station depends a lot on the platforms where you arrive and leave, and whether you know the station and will find it easy to follow the signs that guide you to the platform. As we can see here, literacy also has a spatial element to it and the need to 'navigate' an unfamiliar environment by relying on the written information that is displayed is an important form of everyday literacy.

The above examples demonstrate that travelling by train involves specific literacy and numeracy practices. Particular terms are used and cultural knowledge is required. It is these conventions and assumptions around literacy that make the literacy event work. Travelling by train in Britain, one needs for example to know that, until just before the train arrives, there is a possibility that the platform might be changed. This explains why passengers often do not wait on the platform, but in the departure hall, where they keep their eyes glued to the station monitors waiting for their train to be announced. Any newcomers to travelling by train in Britain – be they foreign visitors, newly arrived immigrants or simply people who do not travel frequently – need to acquaint themselves with these situated literacy practices (Barton, Hamilton and Ivanič 2000).

Much more could be said about train literacies, or the reading and writing that is involved in the social practice of using trains. Think for example about what you do when you get on the train. You know that on some trains the combination of letters and numbers on your ticket tells you where to find your seat. Again, much of this is implicit knowledge. For many of us, train rides are regular events in our lives, they are regular practices, ruled by conventions and rules that we know. We are familiar with the uses of literacy involved in taking a train, and we understand the meanings of timetables, monitors and tickets. The culture-specific nature of these practices may become apparent to us only when on holiday or during a business trip abroad, when we are confronted with a different train system, with timetables that look different from the ones we know and with a fare structure that we are not familiar with.

Now what does it mean to say that literacy is social? In the above example of travelling by train, there are people involved and the social relationships that exist between them. These people are you, your fellow-passengers, the train conductor, the driver and many others. They are involved in particular literacy events. Think for example about what happens when you sit in somebody else's seat, or what the train conductor will do if you do not have a ticket. But the contexts in which literacy and numeracy are embedded are not only social. They are also institutional. In our example of the train, the main institutions involved are the train company, the company that runs the station from where you depart, Network Rail and the Rail Authority. The train company sets the timetable and all you, as the customer, can do is read their timetable and wait patiently for the train to arrive, even if, as ever so often, it is half an hour late. In cases of major delays, you can, however, fill out a complaints form, hoping that your ticket will be reimbursed. I will expand on the role of the institutional context in Chapter 3.

To summarise: the context we refer to, when we talk about literacy as a social practice, consists of people and their intentions (you want to see your mother and you hate taking the car), of actions and interactions, of rules and conventional behaviour, of cultural knowledge and of institutions.

Literacy events and literacy practices

So much for literacy events and the social contexts within which reading and writing takes place. You may still wonder what the term literacy practices refers to.

The term 'practice' can be used in various ways. In everyday use, we might speak about practice as something you do on a regular basis, to either develop or maintain skills, as in 'practising the piano'. Practice is also often contrasted with theory, and this is common in academic as well as non-academic areas. In order to get a driving licence, you need to pass a theory as well as a practical test. As a noun, practice can also refer to an area of work within which people engage in recognisable activities associated with particular bodies of knowledge and expertise, as in the 'practice of medicine' or the 'practice of law'. Practice here refers not only to a profession (lawyer, doctor) but to a domain of social activity that has its particular structures, roles and conventions. Another example would be the social practice of classroom teaching (Fairclough 2003), which is likely (at least to some extent) to be different from the social practice of teaching adults in community settings.

There are two important things to bear in mind about social practices. Firstly, there is something stable or repeated in any social practice. Practices involve recurring patterns of behaviour that are culturally recognisable. For example, the practice of classroom teaching in Britain follows particular conventions and rules, some of which are culturally determined, others institutionally determined. On the other hand, a social practice is never completely fixed. Individual teachers have to implement the rules of the English, Welsh or Scottish school system and are likely to follow the conventions learned in their training and the habits adopted through-out their career (thereby reinforcing these same rules, habits and conventions), but they are also likely to develop their own particular ways of teaching. Every actor who engages in a social practice has the potential to diversify and transform it.

The second important thing to say about social practices is that they involve people making meaning and communicating their meanings, by using language and other semiotic means. Accordingly, social practices include language and they also include discourse (in the sense defined in Chapter 1; see also Fairclough 2003: 122–133). While some common social practices may rely heavily on speech, many contemporary social practices involve the use of written languages.

The term 'literacy practices' draws on the above understanding of social practices. Literacy practices refer to the distinctive ways people engage in social practices that involve reading and writing. In a sense then, literacy practices are those elements of social practices that refer directly to the use of written language. If we come back to classroom teaching, and now think more directly about teaching an adult literacy class, there are likely to be many literacy practices at the core of this social practice. Reading from subject-based textbooks may be a common practice in school classrooms, but not so much in adult classes where a range of materials is used. Individual learning plans, on the other hand, are commonly used in adult literacy, numeracy and ESOL classes in Britain, but they are not common in secondary school classes.

Whether we think of literacy practices as distinctive social practices or consider them to be elements of broader social practices is a matter of degree and emphasis, and to some extent, is irrelevant. In some cases, it may be difficult to clearly identify the literacy elements of a social practice. In other cases, however, we may want to talk about a specific literacy practice that – albeit part of a broader social practice – stands on its own. An example would be the practice of writing Christmas cards. This is also a good example of how literacy practices are culturally shaped, as the habit of giving Christmas cards to your neighbours and work colleagues, which is so common in Britain, is unknown in other European countries. Of course, as a literacy practice, Christmas cards are part of the much broader social and cultural practice of how we celebrate Christmas.

I will now say a few more things about the difference between literacy events and literacy practices. 'Literacy events' refer to what people do with reading and writing: they are the uses of literacy, which can be observed and described. 'Literacy practices' is the more inclusive term, which encompasses both the uses and the meanings of literacy in a particular literacy event. These uses and meanings have to do with learned ways of using reading and writing, with social norms, with values, attitudes and feelings, as well as with social and institutional relationships. Literacy practices refer to these internal processes of the individual as well as to the implicit social and cultural rules and conventions that govern how we behave, what we think and how we relate to each other.

While 'literacy event' is primarily a descriptive concept (what can be observed and recorded by watching people engaging with written language), the term 'literacy practices' moves us into the realm of analysis, trying to understand the meanings of events observed, looking for patterns across events, similarities and differences between them and trying to understand their relationship with other elements of the world. Accordingly, literacy practices refer not only to what people are doing with texts, but include the ideas, attitudes, ideologies and values that inform their behaviour in a literacy event and how they understand what is happening (Baynham and Baker 2002). The term 'literacy practices' can be used not only when referring to the literacy practices of a particular domain of social activity, as in home literacy practices, but also when talking about one particular person's reading and writing.

To summarise, we can say that literacy practices refer to:

- the social activities as part of which we read and write;
- the social and institutional contexts within which reading and writing takes place;
- the cultural conventions and the social rules that govern our behaviour in a literacy event;
- the people who read and write, and the meanings and intentions they bring to this event.

Literacy events and literacy practices are the two basic units of analysis that researchers who adhere to a social theory of literacy use in order to describe what literacy is about. A further term that I have already used is 'literacies' in the plural.

The term 'literacies' is used in several ways. Originally, the term was coined in order to emphasise that reading and writing practices are never exactly the same, but are shaped by the particular social and cultural context within which they take place. If literacy varies with time and place, and is shaped by particular social and cultural practices, it makes sense to abandon the idea of a single literacy. Instead, we can speak about different or multiple literacies (Street 2000). The term 'literacies' can also be used in order to refer to literacies in different languages. We then speak about multilingual literacies (Martin-Jones and Jones 2000). A final thing to say about 'literacies' is that, in practice, the term is similar to the notion of 'literacy practices' and that many researchers use the terms as synonyms.

You will have noticed that while most of the discussion in this text has been concerned with reading and writing, the term 'numeracy' has appeared several times, for example in relation to choosing between different types of train tickets. Numeracy is a frequent component in people's everyday activities and it is often integrated with literacy. It is therefore useful to think of numeracy in a similar way to literacy: as a social practice that is part of people's regular activities (Johnston 1999). Examples of everyday numeracy practices are dealing with invoices and bank accounts, measuring ingredients for a cake, using and recording phone numbers, or playing cards.

The New Literacy Studies (NLS)

The concept of literacy as a social practice was first developed by researchers in the 1980s. These linguists, social anthropologists and psychologists studied the role of literacy in a variety of communities, including people in the South Carolinas (Heath 1983), in Sierra Leone (Scribner and Cole 1981) and in Iran (Street 1984). They were interested in the role of literacy in everyday life. At a time when academics' work on literacy was gathered around the idea of reading and writing as discrete skills whose acquisition was believed to be essential for both the individual's and society's development, such an interest was new.

This was the start of a shift in orientation that led to the development of a new perspective or paradigm. Today, this has developed into a significant body of research known as the New Literacy Studies (NLS). Two things characterise the NLS: firstly, their understanding of literacy as a culturally embedded social practice rather than an individual skill, and, secondly, the move away from educational settings and teaching issues towards an interest in the uses and meanings of literacy and numeracy in people's everyday lives.

The NLS emerged as a reaction to a number of assumptions about literacy that at the time were widespread. Researchers associated with the NLS, many of whom (notably Street) worked in the so-called developing countries, challenged the 'Great Divide' theories of earlier anthropologists, psychologists and economists who claimed that literacy was an important motor of individual and societal development. (For a good introduction to the ideas of the Great Divide theorists, see Collins and Blot 2003.) The Great Divide here refers to the assumed gap between oral and written societies, or, at the individual level, between people who can and those who cannot read and write. Goody (1968, 1986), the most prominent proponent of the Great Divide theory, believed that because literacy allows us to objectify speech and to store and disseminate knowledge in ways that are not possible in purely oral societies, literacy transforms social organisation. Olson (1977, 1994), who was more interested in the consequences of literacy for the individual, claimed literacy to be an important motor for individual cognitive development.

The Great Divide theory has been influential in shaping adult literacy policies worldwide, and in particular in developing countries. It provided the rationale that increased literacy would more or less automatically lead to economic development and societal modernisation, allowing countries to catch up with the progress made in the industrialised countries of the North. Against such views, researchers such as Street and others (see for example Kulick and Stroud 1993, Besnier 1995, Ahern 2001) set their own studies of how people in different cultures, rather than being transformed by literacy, 'take up' literacy and use it for various purposes in the context of their own cultural ways of communication (Kulick and Stroud 1993). Another point of critique was that Goody, Olson and other proponents of the Great Divide ignored the knowledge and understanding of any 'indigenous' communication system (which may be oral or rely on a variety of semiotic means) and any local forms of knowledge and experience that are not codified in writing. Such writing-centred views are now considered ethnocentric and therefore prejudicial.

Street and others also reacted to the limited success of many literacy interventions (among others, the large international programmes such as the UNDP-funded Experimental World Literacy Programme; see Rassool 1999), which by that time had become apparent. Indirectly, these programmes supported their critique of the Great Divide theory, since many of them showed particularly poor results in terms of any significant life changes for those involved.

In North America and Britain, the New Literacy Studies started from a slightly different orientation. Heath (1983), in her seminal study of three communities in the South Carolinas, showed that children in black working-class, white working-class and (black and white) middle-class communities were socialised into very different 'ways with words' or culturally-rooted practices of reading and writing. She was also one of the first researchers to think about the educational implications of her findings, arguing that when middle-class children entered school, they were already familiar with many of the activities that were common in schools. One example is the bedside story that initiates children into ways of taking meaning from texts, which are at the heart of learning and teaching in schools.

In Britain, the NLS have from the start been interested in adults and the way they use reading and writing in their everyday lives. In Lancaster, David Barton, Mary Hamilton and others have been involved in a major research project to study the uses of literacy in different communities (see Barton and Ivanič 1991). *Local Literacies* (Barton and Hamilton 1998) is a study of literacy in one part of Lancaster, and the short reading that accompanies this chapter is an extract from it. Part of the aim of the book is to show the richness and diversity of literacy uses in people's lives and the many meanings literacy has for people. At the same time, the book has been highly influential in exemplifying the kind of ethnographic approach to the study of literacy that I discuss in more detail in Chapter 4.

Because the NLS started primarily as a research perspective, for many years the potential of the social view of literacy for policy and practice remained obscure and links had not been systematically developed. However, there have long been structures in Britain to link research with practice, notably RaPAL (www.literacy. lancs.ac.uk/rapal/rapal.htm). Some of those who consider themselves to be part of the NLS have exchanged views with members of the educational establishment (see Street 1997, MacCabe 1998) and have reacted to new policies (see comment by Barton, Hamilton and Ivanič on the new national curricula for adult literacy and numeracy, www.literacy.lancs.ac.uk/rapal). In recent years, the implications of the social practices view have received much more attention, links with policy have been established and practitioners have started to develop ways of working with adult learners that take up the ideas of the NLS. I discuss these in chapters 5, 6, 7 and 8.

Skills versus practices – two opposing perspectives?

The above discussion may have given the impression that the social practices view denies the nature of reading and writing as skills, which need to be and can be learned. Reading the above sections, you may have come to the conclusion that the skills and the practices view exclude each other. However, while in theory the two perspectives may appear to be exclusive of one another, in practice they should be seen as complementary or perhaps as two approaches, which emphasise different aspects of the reading and writing process. While the skills view highlights the technical and psychological side of literacy, the practices view draws attention to the social and cultural side of it. Where they differ most strongly is with regard to uniformity and diversity. The skills view claims that literacy is a uniform set of skills, while the practices view argues that literacy is not always the same, but differs enormously depending on its social and cultural context of use.

Nevertheless, the social practices view of literacy does not deny the skills of coding and decoding letters and words, which are required for every reading and writing activity. In that sense, it does not exclude the 'technical'. Rather it argues that the technical alone is but one part of what makes up a literacy event: coding and decoding are part of what we do when we read a letter. But how we read it, how we understand its meaning, how we react to it – these have to do with more than skills. In his study of local literacy practices in Bangladesh, Maddox (2001) draws our attention to the very context-specific nature of reading and writing on the marketplace of the Bangladeshi village he worked in. The writing that goes on in the market cannot be understood without also understanding the complex system of borrowing and repaying money that is essential to most market transactions. Yet the mere skills of writing letters and making calculations are of course essential to the market traders' ability to negotiate credits and still make a profit. Maddox (2001: 148) concludes by saying that these economic literacies are, however, quite different from the 'universal' literacy and numeracy skills taught in many adult literacy programmes.

📖 *Reading*

The reading for this chapter consists of extracts from the book *Local Literacies*, a study of everyday reading and writing practices in one community in the north-west of England. Based on ethnographic research carried out at Lancaster, the book provides detailed descriptions of the literacy history and literacy practices of a group of people living in Springside, a district of Lancaster. The authors analyse how these people use literacy in their everyday lives and the significance that written communication has for them, their households and their communities.

Chapter 5 of *Local Literacies* deals with Harry Graham, a pensioner who has lived in Lancaster all his life. Harry had first been contacted as part of a door-to-door survey in Springside. He was visited and interviewed several times by one of the researchers involved in the study that led to *Local Literacies*. Harry comes from a working-class family; his father was a machinist and his mother worked in a canteen. He attended a local infants school and then went on to junior school. Although he passed the exam to enter grammar school, he never went, because his parents couldn't afford to send him. He has always regretted not being able to go to grammar school. He thinks of himself as someone who doesn't have much education ('My education was nil') and contrasts himself with his son, whom he considers to be educated: he went to university and later became a nurse.

During the Second World War, Harry was a seaman in the Royal Navy. Returning from the war, he joined the fire brigade, where he stayed until his retirement. He is a widower and has two children, a son and a daughter, who owns a local hairdresser's.

The extract from Chapter 5 starts with a description of the various literacies Harry makes use of in his daily life. It then goes on to discuss his 'ruling passion' as a way to understand the importance of literacy in Harry's life. There is also a section (not printed here) on Harry's ideas about being educated or uneducated, and the chapter includes several quotes from interviews with Harry as well as extracts from the researcher's notes, each illustrating different aspects of Harry's literacy life. Read through the extract below and discuss the following questions:

- What role(s) does literacy play in Harry's life and why is it important for him.
- What experiences in his life have most strongly influenced his own views about literacy and education?
- Can you think about similar examples from people who you know?

Extract from Barton, D. and Hamilton, M. (1998), 'How they fared in education. Harry's literacy practices', Chapter 5 of *Local Literacies*, London: Routledge, pp. 81–5.

We gradually built up a picture of his life and the role of literacy in it. There are many examples in the transcripts of Harry using different literacies. For a retired person who might be seen as leading a fairly quiet local life he reports a wide range of different literate activities. He has a keen interest in local history and keeps magazines and newspapers associated with this; he spends time reading about this in the library, often taking notes from books. Connected with this he has books, photos and records to do with family history, and says that he and his wife traced his family back to the 1600s, looking up names in church record books and going round cemeteries. He reads a lot, usually about the war and is *never without a book*. Every night he reads in bed for an hour before going to sleep. He only reads *authentic war books*, meaning factual books, and never fiction. He borrows books from the library, going there every Thursday morning, and also buys second-hand books and swaps with friends. Despite not seeing himself as *a writer*, he sometimes writes letters and has written a story for a magazine about his war experiences; during the period we were studying his literacy practices he started writing his life history. Sometimes he refers to writing as *a struggle*, feeling he lacks the necessary training, although at other times he is more positive about it. He always writes letters out in rough first, he is concerned about *proper English*, and sometimes he tears up letters he has written rather than send them.

He uses literacy to keep up with current affairs and local issues. He reads a national daily paper sitting on the settee after breakfast *first thing in the morning, cup of tea and read the paper*. On Fridays he reads the weekly local paper, cutting out and keeping some things for reference. He also reads the local free newspaper which is delivered to the door, church newsletters and the residents' association newsletter, as well as watching television and listening to local radio. Literacy has other roles in his everyday life: his sister does much of his shopping and he keeps money-saving coupons for her to use; reading and writing have a role in organising his finances and paying bills; he has used medical reference books to check on his health, and his son's train timetables to plan holidays; he keeps a diary for future appointments and birthdays; and he takes phone messages for his son who does not have a phone. He helps neighbours with some aspects of literacy, such as helping them with their tax forms, and in turn is helped by others, for example when his son helped him write a job reference for a former colleague.

This kind of help can be seen as part of a complex system of support and reciprocity extending over many years. Within the family, Harry recalls that he began supporting his son's literacy development when he was little. His son would sit on his knee and pick out words from Harry's newspaper, for example: *what we used to do was give him a pen and tell him 'Ring all the "thes" or the "ands"'. That's how he got started, sat down with newspaper.* When his son went to grammar school, he began studying subjects such as Latin which Harry couldn't help him with. So Harry then supported him through finding others *in the circle* who could help him. His wife used to read the children stories, and his son sometimes helped his daughter with her maths. Now Harry's grandchildren often do their homework in his house; neighbours' children often come round and he has sometimes helped them with their homework.

Aside 5.6 Helping others with writing

Oh aye. I've been asked. People come across. 'Will you make me tax form out for me?' And they've fetched all the papers and I've managed the tax forms for them, you know. Things like that.

On reflection I think this was because I was an officer in the Fire Brigade – people must have thought I was an academic, but I got my rank with hard work in studying for the exams, the last and hardest one was when I was fifty-two years old. Well I must be. And I must look the part. I've had people come round for what-do-you-call-its . . . to get a job. References. I've had people come round for references. And I gave them a reference. I gave one lad a reference. He was a fireman and he wanted a job. And he came round to me 'cos I used to be his Officer and asked me for a reference. And I give him one you see. And my lad came round . . . I always take a copy. And my lad come round, who's very well educated and he started laughing at it. I said, 'What's to do?' He said, 'That's no good'. He said, 'You don't do things like that'. And he wrote a proper one out you see. So that I got in my car right away and I took it round to this fellow and I said, 'Give us that one back and have this'.

It was rambling, you see. Instead of getting down to nitty gritty. Oh no, I didn't feel bad about it. No, because what did they expect of me anyway? Well I said, I wrote down what I felt about him and it was all true. So what more do they want. And yet, my lad laughed at it. Well, I read his and he actually said as much in a few words you see. That's what annoyed me. I wish I could do that.

One particular literacy event which is a regular part of his life is that Harry and Ted meet each week on a Wednesday morning to read through and discuss the local newspaper. They sit in the front room of one of their houses, drinking tea and discussing local politics and people they know, *generally putting the world to rights*, as Ted puts it. Sometimes they compose letters to the paper; they plan them together, then Ted writes them out and sends them off. These are *critical contentious* letters aiming to *expand people's opinions a wee bit*. If these letters are accepted by the newspaper, they are published on the letters page of the paper as unsigned anonymous letters coming from *A local resident* or *A taxpayer*. This is a type of letter which is common in local newspapers. These weekly meetings, then, represent a fairly complex literacy event, involving several stages and a range of technologies.

Other current activities he mentions involving literacy include shopping, paying bills, leaving messages, health care, holidays and entertainment. In these activities the networks operate in both directions and are part of broader social patterns of reciprocity. People help Harry and in the same way people have approached Harry for help, with tax forms and other forms. At the working men's club men discuss the war, and sometimes exchange and discuss books and magazines on the subject. This would be part of other networks of support at the club, so, for example, Harry has a friend who mends his car. There are also examples of support at work; when he was in the fire service, a colleague helped him to revise for exams, teaching him the idea of how there is a formula for passing exams, a way of answering questions. Harry used to accompany his wife to graveyards and the library in their search for information about her ancestry. Harry's sister-in-law helps Harry with his shopping sometimes. She takes tokens he has collected for money off various items. She also sometimes walks his dog. When his wife was alive, she and her sister used to shop together.

Having given an overview of Harry's literacy practices, we now turn to making sense of them, looking for patterns and meanings within Harry's practices. In later chapters we will be looking for patterns across different members of the community, and putting them in the explanatory framework of a broader social context. Beginning with making sense of Harry's practices, we will explore them through three themes which appeared prominent in his data.

Ruling passions

The starting-point for understanding Harry and his contemporary practices is the war, the Second World War which he experienced as a young man over fifty years ago. We've called this his ruling passion. He often turned the conversation round to the war; many of his stories were about the war and his interests were linked to it. When we went to interview people *we* wanted to find out about reading, writing and literacy practices. Unfortunately, it seemed, the people we interviewed often wanted to talk about something else; each person had a ruling passion, something *they* wanted to talk about and share with us. We talked to them about literacy, it seemed, and they talked to us about their lives. Often this appeared to have no relation to reading and writing, and we were tempted to say, 'No, don't talk about that: tell us about where you keep your books; tell us if you use the library'. In fact as the interviews continued, we found that when people told us their stories, they ended up telling us much more about literacy.

Examples of Harry's literacy practices which have been given already have links with his ruling passion. He has been reading *authentic war stories* – the phrase recurs – ever since the war finished, joining a number of different libraries in his search for more and more new books on the subject. He discusses and exchanges war books with friends. They are his main reading interest; they have titles like *In Danger's Hour, The Longest Battle, The War at Sea, The British Sailor, Fly for Your Life*.

Harry has also given us interesting information about literacy activities during the war. He kept a diary, although it was confiscated since, for security reasons, service personnel were not allowed to write diaries in wartime. He described the pleasure he got from receiving local newspapers, parcels of pens and paper, and letters from friends and relatives when he was at sea. Letters were sent and arrived in monthly batches. All mail was checked and parts cut out with razor blades. The post took three months to come and the waiting was *unbearable*. He has talked about the letters he wrote home, often written standing while on watch. He found it difficult to write, knowing it would be read by an outsider. Sailors were not allowed to say where they were or what the weather was like; Harry described the coded messages he sent to his mother to describe his location: the first letter of each paragraph spelled out the place where he was. He never told anyone about this and he was never discovered.

In talking about the war Harry speaks of *pumping adrenaline* and the comradeship amongst the men serving. He seems to feel real nostalgia for some aspects of war, but he is also haunted by memories of horror. When he went round the library with Sarah, he pulled a particular book off the shelf and turned to diagrams of a battle he had been involved in; he explained the details to her. (See Aside 5.7.)

Recently, his ruling passion has also motivated Harry to write, in several different ways. He has been trying to make contact with another serviceman who served on the same ship. He has been pursuing this by writing letters to *The Soldier* magazine and a veterans' association magazine. Harry took great care over writing the first letter. It was important to him; he was scared of adopting the wrong tone or failing to communicate what he wanted to say. He rewrote it several times. He has started a correspondence with one old shipmate who wrote an article in one of the magazines.

He also wrote a story for *Landing Craft* magazine. He was invited to do this after attending a meeting of the veterans' association which brings out the magazine. It took him *an hour to write it out, and then about an hour to go through it crossing things out and putting things back in again*. A friend across the road typed it out and he sent it off. It was his first time in print. Part of this article is shown in Aside 5.8 to give an idea of his style of writing.

During our research Harry began to write his own *authentic war story*. When we first talked to him he said he did not enjoy writing at all, but a year later he was surprised to discover that he actually got a great deal of pleasure from writing. He started this partly because of the landing craft article and also has been encouraged

---

Aside 5.7 Diary notes: Harry in the library

We walked past the computer – 'Ever used that?' 'No call to' – and on round the corner to the history section. A small sign at the top of the shelves read WAR STORIES. 'This is where I come . . . nowhere else.' Not wanting to inhibit his search for books I started to browse a bit, half watching him. He has very swift movements. He pulled books out, glanced at the covers, put them back. This went on for about five minutes. Then he pulled one out and started to leaf through it; he appeared to be looking at pictures in it – diagrams and photographs. He replaced it. I pulled out a Laurens van der Post. He came over 'That's a good author', he said. I was surprised. I didn't imagine he'd like someone like that but I didn't comment. 'Mind, it's not a patch on the real stuff – too much writing in it' (it was a slim book) '. . . the author not the people, if you know what I mean.' 'Description?' I asked. 'Yeah, description, that's it. I like the words people said . . . out of their mouths . . . not all this word play, or florification [sic]. There's a lot glorify it.' He was staring at the shelves and pounced on a book. 'I'm in this one.' He flicked through it and found a diagram – some sea battle – lots of lines and little ships. He pointed to one, 'That was me. I was in on that.' I looked at the diagram. I saw a flat line drawing which evoked nothing in me. 'Makes me tingle looking at it,' he said. This is an extreme example of a literacy event which was both shared – we were both looking at a diagram in a book – and, at least at the time, interpreted so differently by the two of us, it could not possibly be called a shared literacy experience.

---

by his son and other people. He is enjoying this kind of writing: *it brings back memories and it's one of the pleasures of my life.* When writing about the war he questions what style he should use: should he keep his story fairly light and amusing for the reader – *there's plenty of humour in war* – or should he describe the darker side and the dirty side of things as well? Would this shock or disturb people? In many ways he needs to make sense of everything that happened. He writes it out by hand and his son will type it for him and will *flower it up a bit . . . not the actual thoughts of the words but flower it up a bit . . . like the dawn broke. It was cloudy, rainy, anything like that, you see.*

The first way of understanding Harry's literacy practices, then, is to locate them in the war, his ruling passion and something not immediately connected with literacy. A second way is to examine how Harry talks about reading and writing, the frames he puts upon it. There are two theories of Harry's which seem to structure his view of literacy; they are the way in which he uses the dimension educated–uneducated and his attitude to reality and fantasy.

Reflection

Answer the following questions for yourself. The questions all have to do with literacy practices of everyday life. The idea is for you to recognise the range of literacies that exist outside classrooms and to begin to think about what literacy means in these contexts.

- Try to remember the last time you had to fill in a form (or, find a form that you can use for the purpose of this exercise): what form was it, who had produced it and for what purpose did you have to fill it out? What did the form look like (think about layout, different fonts, visual aspects, etc.)? Did you have difficulties with it? If so, can you remember what made the form difficult?
- When did you last read or draw a map? Why? What is specific about reading and/or drawing maps compared to dealing with a piece of written language?
- Do you prefer to hand-write or to word-process? How do you think the introduction of computers and mobile phones has changed your own literacy practices?

Research

Have a look at Barton and Hamilton's (2000: 8) six propositions for a social theory of literacy:

- Literacy is best understood as a set of social practices; these can be inferred from events which are mediated by written texts.
- There are different literacies associated with different domains of life.
- Literacy practices are patterned by social institutions and power relationships, and some literacies are more dominant, visible and influential than others.
- Literacy practices are purposeful and embedded in broader social goals and cultural practices.
- Literacy is historically situated.
- Literacy practices change and new ones are frequently acquired through processes of informal learning and sense-making.

Choose a literacy activity that you frequently engage in, or a setting you participate in, which includes the use of texts (a meeting, a classroom, planning a holiday, etc.). Now try to describe the literacy event by using Barton and Hamilton's six propositions. What do they reveal about the literacy practices that are relevant for this event? Do they all apply to your example?

Additional reading

Barton, D. and Hamilton, M. (2000) 'Literacy practices', in D. Barton, M. Hamilton and R. Ivanič (eds) *Situated Literacies: Reading and Writing in Context*, London and New York: Routledge.

Street, B.V. (2000) 'Literacy "events" and literacy "practices": theory and practice in the "New Literacy Studies"', in K. Jones and M. Martin-Jones (eds) *Multilingual Literacies. Reading and Writing Different Worlds*, Amsterdam and Philadelphia: John Benjamins.

Chapter 3

Reading and writing in context

Dominant and vernacular literacy practices

What this chapter is about

How is literacy linked to power and why do some literacy practices have more influence than others? These are the main questions that I discuss in this chapter. At the same time, I pursue in more detail some of the issues regarding a social practice view of literacy that I introduced previously. I begin with a brief discussion of the social patterning of literacy and the relationship of particular literacy practices to different domains of social and institutional life. I then examine the role of power in relation to reading and writing practices in such domains and contexts.

In the last section of the chapter, I begin to discuss the implications of a social practice view of literacy for literacy education. I ask two, related questions. How can a social concept of literacy, numeracy and ESOL help us to better understand what is going on in classrooms and other learning environments? And what literacy practices are being taught and learned there?

The social patterning of literacy: domains of reading and writing

In the previous chapter, I suggested that literacies and numeracies are shaped by the particular social activities and contexts of which they are part. A similar way of putting this is to say that literacies are associated with specific domains of social life (Barton and Hamilton 2000). Such domains are the home or the family, schools or workplaces. Within each domain, literacy is used in particular ways and is shaped by the intentions of those who act in the domain.

Let's take as an example the use of ICT (information and communication technologies). The way electronic technologies are used at work and in people's homes differs and there are various domain-specific genres and literacy practices involving ICT. Overall, at the workplace, the use of computers is structured by the tasks and aims of the company, whereas in the home people use electronic literacies for their own individually determined purposes. At the workplace, e-mails may be used to circulate instructions and work directives. At home, we write e-mails in order to communicate with friends, to keep in touch with relatives who live abroad or to organise a family get-together. The language and style of such texts can vary considerably. Think about the formal language of work directives and the much more colloquial style of personal e-mails and letters.

Following from the above we can say that domains present 'particular configurations of literacy practices' (Barton and Hamilton 2000). In each domain, distinct functions and meanings are attached to literacy. Workplaces prioritise those literacy practices that facilitate the processes and tasks of the particular job in question. This includes the use of specific forms of texts, such as reports, circulars, minutes and others. These are typical genres of the workplace. Another example is the minutes of a meeting that may serve to suggest the course of action to be taken in the coming weeks and to summarise the progress made towards certain goals.

By contrast, notes, diary entries, holiday postcards, magazines and novels are text types that are more likely to appear in home and leisure contexts. What we do with such texts, and the communicative purposes they fulfil are different from the practices associated with texts in work-related contexts. The important point about this is that different domains make use of specific forms of texts, which are embedded in particular forms of communication and social interaction. In other words, they are part of particular practices.

To give yet another example, we can look at the kind of texts we come across in health-care settings. During consultations with their patients, GPs (general practitioners) often type notes into their computers. These notes belong to the patient's personal 'file' that stores all information related to their medical history and any details regarding treatments and medication prescribed. Other types of texts you frequently find in medical settings are the posters displayed in nurses' consultation rooms (typically, these may refer to common diseases or display charts of 'good' and 'bad' foods, inviting you to follow a healthy diet), the leaflets that can be picked up from the waiting-room and the prescriptions you receive from your GP. Such texts are part of the practices and institutional processes of health-care provision.

Boundaries between domains are, however, not clear-cut. While there are fewer and fewer workplaces that do not use ICT, home computers have become increasingly widespread and every day more people get connected to the Internet and the World Wide Web. As a result of this, electronic literacy practices have spread across domains of social practice (Frank 2001). Texts that move between contexts also cut the boundaries between domains (Brandt and Clinton 2002). This happens for example when a patient takes home a leaflet from their nurse and consults it before taking their medication.

The idea of domains as distinct contexts for literacy practices is nevertheless useful if we want to examine the relative status of different literacies across such settings. In the above case, the workplace privileges certain uses of e-mail. In a similar way, health-care settings tend to give authority to particularly literacy practices, mostly those of health-care professionals, and I will come back to this example later in this chapter. Overall, we can say that within the workplace or within institutional settings such as the health-care system, particular literacies have higher degrees of power or influence than others. I will now turn in more detail to literacy's link with power.

Literacy and power: dominant literacy practices

When talking about literacy as a social practice, it is helpful to think about different literacy practices as carrying different degrees of authority or, more simply, as having different degrees of power. In Chapter 1, I discussed different concepts of literacy. As I said then, any attempt to define what literacy is automatically excludes other ways of thinking about reading and writing.

In contemporary societies, schools, further education colleges and institutions of higher education have the authority to define what literacy is. Governments, through these institutions, set standards for what count as appropriate reading and writing practices. On the basis of these standards, they measure literacy levels among the population, they set school examinations and define entry levels for access to professional training and higher education. Schools teach certain forms of literacy. Dictations for example are typical literacy practices of school. Dictations are about norms for correct spelling. They measure to what extent pupils comply with these. Such school literacies (Street and Street 1995) are examples of what are called dominant literacy practices (Barton and Hamilton 1998 and 2000, Prinsloo and Breier 1996). They are backed by the authority of our educational system, which sets standards for what counts as 'proper' literacy.

Academic literacy practices (Jones, Turner and Street 1999, Lea and Stierer 2000) are another example of how institutions select and privilege certain literacies. Think for example about essays and exams, or about academic writing in a broader sense. Academic papers or textbooks are written in a different way than personal letters or novels. They belong to a different genre and they are embedded in particular discourses and institutional procedures. Academic literacy practices set conventions for writing and standards for achievement. They make assumptions about what counts as knowledge and what is scientific. If you do not learn how to write according to these academic standards, you are unlikely to receive good marks for your writing. If you are currently studying for a degree or have recently done so, you will be aware of some of the academic writing practices that are prominent in higher and further education. Essays are a dominant form of literacy in higher education and to a large degree a student's success at university depends on their ability to write essays according to the standards and conventions laid out by their university, their department and their tutors.

However, as Lillis (2001) has pointed out, guidelines on how to write 'good' essays are not always made explicit and they are not necessarily being taught through direct instruction. The resulting uncertainty that characterises many students' experiences with essay-writing has prompted Lillis (2001: 58) to talk about essayist literacy as an 'institutional practice of mystery'. While some students may have had prior experience with writing essays or may find it relatively easy to pick up the rules of the game, others are likely to struggle with this particular form of writing and its associated discourses. An important question with regard to power is whether some students – for example middle-class mainstream students – are in a better position to become successful essay-writers than others. Lillis, who has studied a group of mature students from working-class and/or ethnic minority backgrounds, discusses some of the conflicts these students experience in their attempts to master essayist literacy.

Dominant literacy practices are not confined to educational institutions. My earlier example of electronic literacies has already illustrated that workplaces privilege certain literacy practices. Employers define what literacies are required for particular work-related tasks and specific professions. Such literacies increasingly dominate literacy and education policies in England as well as in other countries. This 'linking of literacy with the economy' (Crowther, Hamilton and Tett 2001: 1; see the reading at the end of this chapter), and with vocational and pre-vocational skills, begins in schools and is extended into adult and community education. In this context, workplace literacies become increasingly dominant. In chapters 5, 6 and 7, I discuss in more detail the changing policy context for adult literacy and numeracy in Britain and the growing role of vocational skills in current adult literacy programmes, replacing the more personal and humanistic learning aims associated with adult education.

An example: literacy and power in health-care contexts

Bureaucratic forms and the rules of how to complete them are another form of dominant literacy practice. Such forms are written in a specific language and they invite specific forms of behaviour. They make use of particular schemes of classification. Forms oblige us to comply with these classifications, as we have to describe our individual personalities and our particular life circumstances within the categories of the institution that stands behind the form (see also Barton 1994: 60–61). We are often reluctant to comply with the requirements of forms. Why, for example, does everybody hate tax forms? Because their layout is confusing, and you never know for sure where you have to put what? Because the rules, on which they are based, are not spelled out? But we also dislike them so much because, as texts, they are the embodiments of the government's authority over a very central part of our lives: our personal finances.

The NHS form to claim support with health-care costs

Fawns and Ivanič (2001) describe six male university students' experiences with the National Health Service HC1 form 'Claim for help with health costs'. This form is for people on a low income to gain help with paying for their health costs. The main purpose of the form is to establish whether the applicant is entitled to such support. Fawns and Ivanič found that the students whose form-filling practices they studied struggled with particular parts of the form. They pondered over the meanings of specific terms. Particular conflicts arose when the answers the form allowed did not match the students' actual circumstances. One student struggled how to answer a question about any 'savings' he might have. Since he had just received a loan of £7500, he included this, but then did not know how to explain that this amount, although in his bank account, was not a saving.

The power of the form is perhaps most visible in the intrusive questions it asks about the applicant's personal financial situation (Fawns and Ivanič 2001). It is also apparent in the complex language it uses and the limited space it provides for applicants to describe their situation in ways that reflect how they experience it. While forms such as NHS HC1 lack such space, they often contain an opening paragraph warning applicants that they have to complete the form as honestly as possible and must not omit any aspect of their circumstances. The hidden threat contained in this statement reveals the power of the form as an institutional literacy practice.

The NHS form (and the students' experience with it) is a particularly telling example of the power a particular text – and the practices that surround it – can have. The form serves as a gatekeeper, regulating access to crucial resources. Whether applicants understand or don't understand it, whether they provide the expected answers and place them in the order provided by the format and layout of the document or not, is likely to be crucial in determining the outcome of their request. As the above example shows, difficulties that arise when filling out a form are not simply a matter of coding and decoding. How otherwise can we explain that students – who undoubtedly can read and write – struggle with this specific literacy practice?

Fawns and Ivanič's example shows that it is worthwhile to take a close look at the institutions that produce forms (in their case the NHS). Different texts make greater or lesser effort to appeal to potential readers. The unappealing nature of the NHS HC1 form may serve the hidden purpose of deterring non-serious applicants. By contrast, the application form of a credit-card provider is likely to be designed in a much more inviting way, reflecting the commercial intent of its producer.

A consultation with a general practitioner

In institutional contexts such as the NHS, texts are not powerful only because of what they say and how they are designed, but also because of the role they take in the processes of health-care provision and in the interaction between doctors and patients. Power is located in the texts (in their language, format, etc.), but also in the way they are used and the role they take on in specific situations. This is illustrated by Freebody and Freiberg's (1999) account of a consultation between an elderly patient and her doctor as a literacy event.

The patient has come to the doctor to get a new prescription for the headache medication she has been taking for quite some time. Talk during the conversation centres around her request and the doctor's hesitation at writing the prescription. At various instances during the consultation, the doctor refers to and makes use of written language. Talking to the patient, he consults his own records on her case, visible to him, but not to her, on his computer screen. His notes reveal that the patient has received a high amount of her medication only recently and should not be in need of a new prescription. Nevertheless, he writes the prescription. While he produces the document, the patient puts forward a request for a different, stronger medication, which the doctor however ignores.

At the beginning of the consultation, the doctor talks to the patient about research that has shown that in the majority of cases headaches are caused by stress. This may seem to be an innocuous remark, but looking at it more closely you can see this as another instance of the doctor relying on his privileged knowledge and referring to an authority that is contained in written language (medical studies are disseminated through published journal articles and reports). Although not physically present (other than perhaps through the thick volumes of medical books that are likely to be placed on the shelves in the doctor's consultation room), written text here has power (through the knowledge it contains). Crucially, power is located not only in the text, but also in the practices that surround it: the doctor does not share texts – such as his patient's record or the studies he refers to – with the patient. He expects her to trust his professional knowledge and judgement. We can see here that power is located in the institution itself, and the position doctors and patients take within it. The institutional context in which the consultation takes place constructs the encounter as a 'medical space' (Fairclough 2001: 49), which legitimises the doctor's language and knowledge.

Power relations (and the role of literacy with regard to them) are of course not fixed and it is possible to imagine a different scenario to the above consultation. Imagine a patient, suffering from migraine over several years, arriving at her doctor's surgery armed with a handful of printouts from the internet and requesting her doctor to change her current medication to a new product that – according to the information she has consulted – is more likely to ease her pain. Again, it is highly revealing to examine this scenario as a literacy event and much could be said about the potential power dynamics in such a case and the role that texts and practices play within it.

The ideological model of literacy

The purpose of the examples discussed in the previous sections was to illustrate how literacy practices are linked to institutional contexts and power structures in society. Powerful social institutions support 'powerful literacies' (Crowther, Hamilton and Tett 2001; see Reading, p. 54). Individuals and groups who possess these literacies are likely to have an advantage over those who don't. Literacy practices are not evenly distributed in society and some groups have easier access to literacy (and education generally) than others. Those who are excluded from powerful literacies do not have the kind of formal qualifications that enable entrance into high-status professions. They may have limited access to public services and they may find it difficult to make use of the benefits they are entitled to.

Researchers who associate themselves with the social view of literacy argue that literacy is not neutral, as the autonomous model suggests, but ideological (Street 1993: 2001). Ideology here is not meant in the sense of dogma or 'false consciousness', but relates to processes of power and domination. Ideologies are ways of thinking about particular aspects of the world and of society that are brought forward by specific groups and individuals in society. They serve to confirm and extend the power-base of this group. Ideologies easily become naturalised, that is, they are accepted as common everyday knowledge though in fact they are part of particular worldviews. Talking about literacy as ideological draws our attention to the role of reading and writing practices in the reproduction of structures of power and domination in society and in the process of social differentiation. Educational institutions, including adult basic education programmes, are centrally involved in such processes.

Dominant literacies make use of dominant languages, and by doing so disempower all those who do not master these dominant idioms. Bureaucratic literacy practices such as public service forms are usually written in English. They need to be filled out in English. This poses particular challenges to the many people living in Britain whose first language is not English.

The term 'dominant literacy practice' – and its opposite, 'local or vernacular literacy practices' – can help us to see how literacy and power relate in practice. Local or vernacular literacy practices are the ways 'ordinary' people use reading and writing and the theories of literacy they hold. Local literacies are different from institutionalised literacy practices. They may include literacy in a different language or dialect (Martin-Jones and Jones 2000), in which case we talk about multilingual literacies. Vernacular literacies (see also Camitta 1993) are associated not with institutional culture, but with the everyday processes of communities. They relate to people's own uses of literacy (e.g. writing graffiti or organising a meeting of the allotment association), and are grounded in people's own discourses about literacy.

A good example of such vernacular literacy practices is the use of literacy mediators. The practice of literacy mediation has been widely studied (see examples in Barton and Hamilton 1998, Baynham and Lobanga Masing 2000, Jones 2000a and b, Kalman 1999). It touches upon the collaborative nature of much vernacular reading and writing. Another example – once again taken from the health-care contexts – is when a patient shares experiences with a particular drug by adding their comments to a discussion site or an internet news group.

To sum up this section on literacy and power, I have put together (below) a list of the main instances where we can find power in relation to particular literacy practices. For analytical purposes, I have separated power in texts from power in practices. In the reality of a literacy event (a text being used in a particular context), these layers are not separate, but are experienced simultaneously.

Power is found in texts in:

- the language the text uses (vocabulary, style, grammar);
- layout and format;
- how the text speaks about people and their experiences (also, who it speaks about, and who is excluded);
- what knowledge is accepted (e.g. professional 'expert' knowledge only?).

Power is found in practices in:

- how the text assigns roles to participants and what behaviour it prescribes (or attempts to prescribe);
- the text's role in the interaction between those involved in the literacy event;
- the text's role in institutional processes (e.g. setting rules and norms for how things are supposed to be done; initiating action and procedures; financial or legal implications).

The items on this list are useful to look at when studying the role of literacy in various contexts of everyday life, using research methods such as participant observation and interviewing. In Chapter 4, I give a brief introduction to such research methods and how they can be applied to the study of literacy as a social practice.

Multilingual literacy practices

In the previous section I have already referred to the role of different languages with regard to literacy. This is a good moment to say a few more things about the relationship between languages and literacies and the contribution that studies of multilingual communities and settings have made to our understanding of the nature of literacy as social practice. A particularly good collection of such studies is published in Martin-Jones and Jones 2000. The contributions to this volume, taken from different geographical and linguistic contexts, are proof that power relations inevitably characterise the relationship between different languages and different literacies.

These relations of inequality are grounded in historical contexts, present-day economic and political relations and patterns of migration that result in people leaving their primary linguistic environment and entering new social worlds in which new languages and language variations dominate. Historical contexts go back to the role of colonial regimes but also to the relationships between different groups of one society (for example the British) and the significance of regional dialects in our own history. There is a close link here between political and economic contexts (e.g. the subordinate position of colonised people) and linguistic and cultural rights.

In contemporary societies, including the British, multilingualism is no longer an exception but a reality. Understood in a broad sense, the concept of multilingualism covers not only different languages, but also different dialects and scripts. Jones (2000a and b) has written about Welsh speakers in rural communities who speak a regional variety of Welsh, as well as a regional variety of English, and who read and write standard English. Saxena (1993) has researched the language and literacy practices of three generations of a Panjabi Hindu family living in London. His account is evidence of the complex nature of the family's linguistic repertoire, and the richness of their linguistic experiences and competences, something that is frequently ignored in educational contexts. The five family members in Saxena's study (grandparents, parents and their 4-year-old child) together speak, read and write four languages and four scripts. These languages and scripts serve different communicative purposes and the family members constantly make choices of what language to use, when and what for.

More importantly for this chapter, Saxena's examples tell us a lot about the situational power of specific literacies and languages. An example is the role of Hindi in the local Hindu temple, where the father is a member of the temple executive committee. The committee drafts a letter addressed to the temple members in English. However, they agree that, if they had more funds, they would prefer to produce a bilingual letter. The committee uses handwritten notices in Hindi to place on the temple noticeboard. We can see that in the context of the Hindu temple (even in the middle of London) English is of limited use and has limited power. In other contexts, however, it is English that is most valued and that is required of each participant in a literacy event. When the mother takes her son to nursery school, she picks up a note from the teacher – written in English – about an activity she and her son were involved in. The mother's ability to read English is essential for successful communication with her son's school.

Saxena's family must be regarded as linguistically privileged – they have access to a wide range of communicative resources, which allow them to operate meaningfully in a variety of contexts, including those that require standard English. This is not necessarily the case for ethnic communities living in England. Individuals are often restricted in their access to privileged literacies. Such constraints become most apparent in educational contexts – when students lack access to the dominant literacy practices of the classroom and are branded as under-achievers, while their own literacies are ignored or marginalised as 'non-standard' and vernacular forms of literacy. Finally, particular groups within one community may be denied access to dominant literacies. Among some migrant groups, women have much less opportunity to learn English than men. In such cases, lack of literacy is symbolic of men's dominance over women and gaining access to literacy can become an important factor in women's struggle for greater independence (see Rockhill 1993).

Implications of the theory of literacy as social practice for adult language, literacy and numeracy education

What happens when we apply the theory of literacy as a social practice to educational contexts? The social practices view of literacy starts from the assumption that, in order to understand what is going on in a classroom, we need to know how people use reading and writing in everyday life. It presumes that in contemporary societies even those who (according to official statistics) are illiterate are involved in much reading and writing on a day-to-day basis. Accordingly, the social theory of literacy is interested in what people do with literacy in everyday life and, more generally, in the role literacy has in their lives. People write postcards when they are on holiday, because they want to tell friends about the great time they had on their summer break in Blackpool. Other people complete application forms because they want to have a credit card. In a literacy class, learners read word lists, they add missing words to sentences or they practise writing a letter because they want to improve their spelling, learn new words or learn how to write on a computer.

If literacy is always situated in a social and institutional context and is shaped by the intentions of those who use it, the same must also be true for literacy in educational contexts. In the above examples, learners have reasons why they spend their time struggling to spell words. They have their own personal goals, and literacy for them is important insofar as it relates to these aims. At the same time, the organisers of the literacy class, and its teachers, pursue their own goals. Crucially, these goals shape what is being taught in the class. Have a look at the following example.

For more than 18 years, Wendy, a 42-year-old woman, worked in social care. Two years ago, after a dispute with her employer, she lost her job. Since then, she has not been employed again, although she could have easily found another job as a carer. Wendy does not want to go back into social care. But it is difficult for her to find another job. She would like to become a receptionist. However, her spelling is bad and she does not know how to use a computer. Nowadays, every receptionist needs to be able to work on a computer. This is why Wendy has joined a literacy class that takes place twice a week in a further education college in the north-east of England. Her teacher, Patricia, has been working as a basic education tutor for almost 20 years. Patricia wants to help Wendy achieve her goal. Patricia develops individual learning plans for each of her students. These consist of particular literacy practices; in Wendy's case for example, there is a lot of work on words that have similar pronunciations, but different spellings. Besides having problems with her spelling, Wendy is a confident reader and writer. She is used to dealing with invoices and she coped with all the paperwork relating to her court case.

There are ten regular students in Patricia's class. Each of them has come to the class with specific literacy-related problems and every student spends the two hours of the class working on particular literacy practices. Ben, a builder and currently unemployed, is working on his CV. Matthew, 17 years old, is training to become a chef. Matthew is dyslexic and his course leaders sent him to the basic education class in order to improve his writing. As many other people of his age, Matthew is an avid writer of text-messages. He spends his free time writing songs and inspired by his mother's new partner, who is Chinese, he has recently begun to learn the Chinese alphabet.

U. Papen, 'Learners in an adult basic education class in a further education college in the north east of England' (June 2002), unpublished.

Learners in adult literacy, numeracy and ESOL classes are involved in a range of personal and family-related literacy practices. Like Matthew, they may have difficulties with some forms of literacy, but are highly skilled in others. This is also the case with ESOL learners, many of whom may be 'illiterate' in English, but highly literate in their own language. Others may even master several languages and scripts. Many adults come to literacy and numeracy classes wanting help with particular literacy practices. Others, however, have more general aspirations. What learners will be taught and what they will learn are specific types of reading and writing. These literacy practices, however, are part of broader educational aims and therefore are shaped by the norms, values and practices of the educational programme and the institutions that fund it. I discuss these issues in more detail in chapters 5, 6 and 7.

We may now want to ask some questions about the implications of a social theory of literacy for literacy education. I will come back to these questions in Chapter 8.

- From a social literacies perspective, what needs to be included in literacy education?
- How do people switch between the literacy practices required in different contexts?
- How can we create links between people's own literacies and the literacy practices of schools, bureaucracies and workplaces?
- How can local literacies and multilingual literacies be validated, that is, be given more space in educational and institutional settings?
- How do people's own conceptions of literacy and their own experiences of literacy/education in society orientate them towards particular types of literacy programmes?

📖 *Reading*

This reading comes from a collection of articles that originated in a conference organised by RaPAL (Research and Practice in Adult Literacy) and the University of Edinburgh. RaPAL, a network of researchers and practitioners, aims to improve links between research and practice, and to provide a forum for the critical debate of current policies and practice in adult literacy, numeracy and ESOL.

The articles published in *Powerful Literacies* all conceptualise the link between co-existing but unequally powerful literacy practices. While some papers discuss the effects that dominant literacy practices have on those who do not easily have access to them, other chapters describe adult literacy programmes that aim to support vernacular literacies and to empower learners. The reading is the start of the book's Introduction.

Crowther, J. Hamilton, M. and Tett, L. (2001) 'Powerful literacies: an introduction', in J. Crowther, M. Hamilton and L. Tett (eds) *Powerful Literacies*, Leicester: NIACE, pp. 1–4.

The inspiration for this book originated from a conference sponsored by *RaPAL* and the University of Edinburgh on the theme of powerful literacies. The aim of *RaPAL* is to bring together researchers and practitioners as a way of ensuring that all are informed by developments in their respective fields of work. The Edinburgh conference did just that. It attracted participants from across the UK and also internationally, whose voices can now be heard in this collection. This book has another origin too – but this time a far less positive one. At the beginning of the twenty-first century the issue of literacy (in schools as well as in adult education) dominates the policy agenda in 'developing' as well as 'over-developed' countries. The linking of literacy with the economy and the impact of literacy league tables, as constructed by the International Adult Literacy Surveys, have been powerful forces that have shaped the literacy debate and our understanding of the issues involved. The opportunity for thinking about what literacy means and the issues it involves for developing alternative practices has been squeezed out by the demands of government and global corporations preoccupied with narrowly conceived ideas of human resource development. The space for another vision needs to be created. What is missing is the experiences of practitioners, researchers and broader understandings of literacy and how people use it in everyday ways. The purpose of this book is to contribute towards opening a space for divergent and critical voices to be heard; ones that are grounded in research and practice into the meanings of literacy and what it means to work with literacy students.

Before we can speak about powerful literacies we need to set it against the dominant assumptions made about adult literacy practice. The dominant model systematically fails to address issues of power relations in people's lives and what they can do about them. The selection and distribution of literacy to different social groups is not something that happens neutrally, as it were, above the interests that pattern society. Instead, they are embedded in its infrastructure of power relationships. Literacy is deeply and inescapably bound up with producing, reproducing and maintaining unequal arrangements of power.

The literacy ladder

Definitions of what it means to be literate are always shifting. It is socially constructed and cannot be seen outside of the interests and powerful forces that seek to fix it in particular ways. The common way to think about literacy at the moment is by seeing it as a ladder that people have to climb up. This begins in schooling and adult literacy is the extension of the process in post-school contexts. The emphasis is, therefore, on standardising literacy accomplishments, tests, core skills, and uniform learning outcomes that are specified in advance of the learning process. People are ranked from bottom to top with the emphasis on what they can't do rather than what they can. This leads to a deficit model where those on the bottom rungs are positioned as lacking the skills that they need. Moreover, adults are seen as '[not] even vaguely motivated to do something about their own plight' (Tester, 2000: 42). The frameworks used to define this ladder are top-down ones constructed largely in terms of pre-vocational and vocationally relevant literacy requirements. Consequently, they do not recognise the validity of people's own definitions, uses and aspirations for literacy so they are 'disempowering' in the sense that they are not negotiable or learner-centred and not locally responsive. They define what counts as 'real literacy' and silence everything else. If, however, the emphasis is put on how adults can and want to use literacy then the focus moves to what people have, rather than what they lack, what motivates them rather than what is seen as something they need.

New research and practice has been at the forefront of undermining the conceptual adequacy of the discourse of deficit. It does so by grounding literacies in a social and ecological context. They are no longer disembodied skills but aspects of real people's lives in everyday situations. What has become known as the New Literacy Studies (as in Gee, 1990; Street, 1996; Barton, 1994; Barton and Hamilton, 1998) uses an approach which sets out from a different point – starting from the local, everyday experience of literacy in particular communities of practice. Its approach is based upon a belief that literacy only has meaning within its particular context of social practice and does not transfer unproblematically across contexts; there are different literacy practices in different domains of social life, such as education, religion, workplaces, public services, families, community activities; they change over time and these different literacies are supported and shaped by the different institutions and social relationships. Detailed studies of particular situations can be revealing about these differences and in turn these help identify the broader meanings, values and uses that literacy has for people in their day-to-day lives. We would argue that any research that purports to increase our understanding of literacy in society must take account of these meanings, values and uses – and indeed they are the source of the ideas which statisticians use to interpret their findings. The new literacy studies dispenses with the idea that there is a single literacy that can be unproblematically taken for granted. We have to begin to think in pluralistic terms about the variety of literacies that are used in different contexts in order to make meaning – and in order to make literacy practice meaningful to people.

New modes and conventions for communicating through information and communication technologies are also raising issues about what counts as 'real' literacy. The juxtaposition of icons, imagery and text is presenting new challenges for the process of communication and the literacies associated with it (see Street, this volume). In an information-rich world there is an increasing gap between those with access to information and those denied it. Redistributing information and making it accessible to the 'information poor' is an important educational and political task. Moreover, the demands of a 'knowledge economy' and an 'information society' cannot simply be constrained within the traditional conventions of literacy understanding. Its development exposes the inadequacy of current thinking that constitutes literacy as externally defined rungs on a ladder that has been designed as an extension of initial schooling, rather than in terms of the real shape of literacy practices and goals in adult life. Rather than seeing literacy as a tool for organising our knowledge that is consistent with the economistic vision of the global economy, we need other ways of conceptualising literacy that can embody more democratic visions.

Making power visible

Power that is recognisable is also negotiable (Melucci, 1988: 250)

Literacy that obscures the power relations inscribed in its construction ultimately disempowers. It treats as technical what is in fact socially and politically constructed and is therefore misleading. In one sense, therefore, powerful literacies have to be oppositional. They have to open up, expose and counteract the institutional processes and professional mystique whereby dominant forms of literacy are placed beyond question. They have to challenge the way 'literacy' is socially distributed to different groups. They have to reconstruct the learning and teaching process in a way that positions students in more equal social and political terms. In another sense they should be propositional, in that they have to construct alternative ways of addressing literacy practices and interests grounded in real lives and literacy needs.

They need to be critical and political too. The agenda for developing powerful literacies has to be informed by issues of social justice, equality, and democracy in everyday life rather than be limited to a narrow, functional definition primarily addressed to the needs of the economy.

Researchers and practitioners have to construct alliances in order to develop their own agency to act back on the forces that seek to shackle them to a narrow and impoverished vision of literacy. Powerful literacies involve constructing a curriculum that enables workers to learn and share experience. This acts as a counter force against the powerful forces that have dominated the literacy discourse. Increasingly, the stage for these alliances has to be global as well as local. The forces that are impacting on literacy practice are – as many of the accounts here demonstrate – not restricted to national boundaries. Powerful literacies involve opening up the many voices that are silenced in dominant definitions of literacy. It involves people deciding for themselves what is 'really useful literacy' and using it to act, individually and collectively, on their circumstances to take greater control over them. Literacy is a resource for people acting back against the forces that limit their lives. Whilst literacy has to be understood broadly in that it involves social processes of making and communicating meanings, the importance of textual communication always figures prominently. It involves learning to be critical readers and writers in order to detect and handle the inherently ideological dimension of literacy, and the role of literacy in the enactment and production of power (see Lankshear et al., 1997).

Powerful literacies speak to an agenda informed by concerns to extend the autonomy of individuals and communities that have been marginalised and ignored. The emphasis is shifted from literacy as a deficit in people to an examination of the literacy practices that people engage in that recognises difference and diversity and challenges how these differences are viewed in society. The deficit, if there is one to be located, is in a society that excludes, reduces and ridicules the rich means of communication that exist amongst its people. The policy discourse both within the UK and the wider world is premised on a basic skills model that prioritises the surface features of literacy and language and we show, through a variety of contexts and practices, how inappropriate this is.

Reflection

Read the extract printed above and discuss the following questions:

- What does the term 'powerful literacies' mean?
- Look at possible interpretations of the term contained in the reading.
- Can you think about examples of literacies that play a powerful role in your own or in your family's and friends' lives?

Research

If you are a teacher of literacy, numeracy or ESOL, how do you think about the link between literacy and power in your own work? Try to identify examples from your own experience that reveal the role of power in relation to literacy (numeracy and/or ESOL).

Additional reading

Prinsloo, M. and Breier, M. (1996) (eds) *The Social Uses of Literacy*, Amsterdam: John Benjamins, pp. 11–33.

Street, B.V. (2001) 'Introduction', in B.V. Street (ed.) *Literacy and Development: Ethnographic Perspectives*, London: Routledge, pp. 1–19.

Chapter 4

Using ethnography to study literacy in everyday life and in classrooms

What this chapter is about

The change from a skills-based model of literacy and numeracy to an understanding of reading, writing and calculating as social practices has important implications for how we can study literacy. The social theory of literacy suggests that, in order to understand what literacy is about, it is best to look at how it is used. It suggests that we need detailed accounts of what people actually do with reading and writing, and the meanings literacy has in particular contexts. In this short chapter, I explain how we can produce such accounts. This chapter contains a brief introduction to the use of ethnography – a qualitative research methodology – to study literacy and numeracy. At the end of the chapter, I suggest a research exercise that you can carry out on your own, which will allow you to try out some of the research methods described here.

What is ethnography?

Ethnography refers to close, in-depth examinations of social activities as they occur in real-life settings. The term can also be used to designate the written product of ethnographic research, in which case we talk about *an* ethnography. Ethnography was first developed by social anthropologists who studied the lives of communities different from their own. Bronisław Malinowski (1922), widely regarded as one of the founding fathers of modern ethnography, who proclaimed that, if anthropologists were serious about understanding other people's cultures, they had to learn their language, live with them over a considerable period of time and take part in their everyday life.

Malinowski's story is simple. He came from Poland, and first planned a career in science, but later came to the London School of Economics to study social anthropology. When the First World War broke out, he was about to begin anthropological research in Australia. As an Austrian citizen, he was regarded as an enemy alien, to be interned. Thanks to the generosity of the Australian authorities, he was allowed to spend his internment on the Trobriand Islands, a remote archipelago in the Pacific. Out of necessity, he began his fieldwork: isolated from contact with other Europeans, he lived among the local population, learned their language and began to participate in their lives, while at the same time observing what was happening around him. Participant observation as a method of study was born. When the war was over, Malinowksi returned to England and wrote his monographs about the Trobriander. On the basis of his experiences, he formulated the principles of participant observation and ethnographic fieldwork, which from the 1920s onwards became the standard anthropological research method.

Contemporary ethnography

Since then, much has changed. Malinowski's methods have been adapted by researchers from within anthropology, sociology, education research and other social science disciplines. Ethnography (or 'fieldwork', as it is also called) is nowadays a qualitative research methodology, widely used across the social science disciplines. From its original, rather rigid and demanding framework, it has changed into a variety of approaches and it is often combined with other qualitative and quantitative methods. One of the main characteristics of contemporary ethnography is that it is much more flexible in its subject choice. Malinowski and his followers set out to study cultures as a whole, and in many ways what they attempted to do was to construct a pure (and perhaps idealised) picture of the culture in its natural state of being, untouched by historical developments and the broader social and economic conditions related to the advent of colonialism. The classical anthropologists believed that participant observation was able to provide an objective and 'true' picture of the culture and the people they were studying. From their perspective, the influence of the researcher in the field was to be eliminated as far as possible.

Needless to say, contemporary ethnography takes issue with most of these ideas. First of all, ethnography is no longer solely used for the study of entire communities and their ways of life. More selective approaches are common. Most contemporary ethnographies will look at only one aspect of a community's social world, and this could be people's reading and writing practices. Rather than studying whole cultures, ethnic groups or sub-cultures, the location of the ethnography may be a factory, a school, a neighbourhood, a group of students or an adult literacy class. While long-term fieldwork of the kind Malinowski carried out may still be the ideal for many ethnographers, nowadays the approach is also used for more short-term research projects, which can include several localities or fieldsites (what Marcus calls multi-site ethnography; see Marcus 1998).

I said earlier that Malinowski believed ethnography to be an 'objective' or realist method. Today, most ethnographers have abandoned such a view and situate themselves in an interpretive or critical paradigm. How they approach their research is related to their understanding of what the social world – the object of their research – is like. Researchers are now more aware of their beliefs about the nature of social reality – their different ontologies, we might say – and the epistemological question: how valid is this knowledge? How can they find out about the social world and the people who, as I would say, make this world or are this world?

Ontology and epistemology cannot be separated from one another. If you believe the social world to be something that is governed by structures and regularities, which can be explained by isolating specific factors and observing the correlations between them, as a researcher you will use instruments such as surveys, experiments or tests. If, however, you believe that social phenomena emerge from a multitude of factors, which interact with each other to produce different effects in different contexts, you need research methods that examine social phenomena in all their respective contexts and are able to take into account multiple and overlapping factors.

Thinking about language (spoken and written) and about culture as two more specific aspects of the social world that linguists and literacy researchers are concerned with, similar questions need to be asked. What is language? What is culture? As literacy researchers, are we interested in written language as an abstract system of signs, or are we thinking about language as it is used by people for purposes of meaning-making and communication? For those who adhere to a social practices view of literacy, formal linguistic analysis is unlikely to yield any significant insights. We need research methods that can gauge the role written texts play in actual interactions, in 'real life' contexts.

As to culture, contemporary social scientists would not agree with the early anthropologists' static idea of culture as a kind of blueprint or model according to which a community organises its social world and decides what to believe in. Rather, culture today is understood as a continuous process of meaning-making (Hall 1997), emphasising the role of people as active agents in constructing the social world they live in. Culture in that sense is a process rather than a product, and any attempt to study culture needs to focus on the people and the social practices through which culture is being produced. Language, in this view, is part of culture and it is equally subject to individual and communal change. A research method that is particularly suitable to the study of language and culture as dynamic and 'real' processes is ethnography.

How to do ethnography

Ethnographic research draws its data from the observation of, and participation in, everyday life events. Since it emphasises the role of people as active agents in the construction and negotiation of social reality, it privileges research methods such as interviews and participant observation over structural analysis. Most importantly, since ethnography is grounded in the idea of the social world as being complex and fluid, it believes that what can be grasped at the surface of social phenomena cannot provide us with satisfying explanations about what causes things to happen and what makes people act in one way or the other. In order to find such explanations, the researcher needs to understand the situation and its context. She needs to spend time talking to the people who are part of it and to ask them about their experiences of the situation in question. The core of ethnography's claim to validity is its grounding in the close interaction of the researcher with her research subjects and the intersubjective understanding that is developed in the course of fieldwork (Davies 1999). It is on this basis that ethnography claims to be much better placed to understand social phenomena (in all their complexity) than, for example, survey methods.

To summarise, the term ethnography refers to a particular form of qualitative research, which is based on certain principles and uses a range of research techniques. The principles that ethnography is grounded in are these:

- Ethnography is holistic (not isolating individual factors).
- It includes engagement in the lives (or in selected aspects of the lives) of those being studied, usually over longer periods of time.
- It studies real subjects in real-life contexts.
- It draws out the insiders' (emic) perspective.
- It is based on an interpretive process that involves both the researcher's and the research subjects' perspective on the issues in question.

The main research techniques (or research methods) that ethnography applies are:

- participant observation;
- interviews (unstructured, semi-structured and, occasionally, structured in the form of questionnaires and surveys);
- document analysis;
- visual methods (photography, videos, film and the like).

Why ethnography is a suitable method to study literacy as social practice

Having read the above, you may already have guessed that I am now going to suggest that ethnography is particularly suited as a research method in the study of literacy. Let me try to explain how this choice of method relates to the theory that informs our thinking about literacy.

Previously in this chapter, I mentioned different ways of thinking about and studying language. Sociolinguists, social anthropologists and many other social scientists are interested primarily in studying language in use. Literacy studies, a field of research at the interface between these disciplines, are concerned with the role of written language in society. Such studies regard literacy not just as a skill, but also as a social practice used in particular contexts for specific aims. Now, if literacy is a social practice, it needs to be studied as such. This means that the researcher who is interested in literacy needs to examine what people do with literacy, when and where this happens and to what ends they use written texts. Furthermore, if literacy is also a 'situated' practice (Barton, Hamilton and Ivanič

2000), we need to study literacy in the contexts in which it is embedded. This is to say that ethnography – with its focus on people, its interest in real-life contexts and its holistic approach – is particularly suited to the study of literacy as social practice.

The use of ethnography to study literacy centrally has to do with the New Literacy Studies' interest in understanding the role of reading and writing in everyday life, rather than just observing the way it is taught and learned in educational settings. Researchers and educationists who consider literacy to be primarily a skill may not share this interest and they are likely to use other methods. A skills perspective orientates researchers towards a focus on testing and measuring literacy levels and on educational experiments (e.g. trying out new teaching methods). By contrast, the New Literacy Studies have led researchers to move away from such questions and to shift their attention to the uses and meanings of literacy in everyday life. This change of focus is ideally matched by ethnography's interest in broader contexts of cultural and social life and by the methodology's traditional focus on people and their meanings (what is called the emic view). As part of this move, ethnographic studies of literacy (or ethnographies of literacy, as they are called) are primarily interested in what people do with literacy, as well as what meanings it has for them in their lives. The Reading in Chapter 2 is an extract from such an ethnography of literacy.

A final thought to add here is that such ethnographies have looked not only at people who can read and write, but also at those who are often claimed to be 'illiterate' or to lack basic skills. This is important because such studies have made us aware that the so-called illiterates (who are the targets of governmental and non-governmental efforts to improve basic skills among the population) are also involved in literacy events and that they have developed their own strategies to deal with written language (see for example Kell 1996). They also have views on what literacy means in their lives and why (or why not) they need to improve their reading and writing.

You can see from the above how theory, topic and method are inter-related. To give an example, in their research in Lancaster, Barton and Hamilton (1998) started with an orienting theory, which was the idea of literacy as social practice. This triggered their interest in a particular topic: the role of reading and writing in the everyday lives of people in a town in the north-west of England. This fairly general interest further led them to explore a range of areas and settings, such as the role of reading and writing in the activities of an allotment association, the production of a newsletter or the role of reading and writing about the war in one particular person's life. Barton and Hamilton's orienting theory (of literacy as social practice) also implied a methodology. Since they needed to find out when, where, and to what ends people in their chosen community in Lancaster used and produced written texts, they had to spend a lot of time finding out about people's lives, about the different activities that took up people's time and about the things that concerned them or that they struggled with. Most importantly, they had to find out what the role of literacy was within these areas. The best way to do this was through asking people about their lives (using interviews) and by participating in selected aspects of their informants' everyday activities.

Participant observation as a method is a useful tool to identify the role of written language in particular contexts and as part of particular activities – let's say, during a meeting of the allotment association (see Barton and Hamilton 1998). However, participant observation on its own can tell you relatively little about why things are done the way they are and why people act in the way you observe. In a sense, participant observation – on its own – limits you to the visible and observable elements of literacy, or, to put it differently, to the literacy events. If you want to understand the practices that bear upon the event, you need to make use of other techniques. You need interviews to help you find out what the people involved in the literacy event think about the reading and writing that is going on, how they interpret the event and what assumptions and beliefs they bring to it. You are also likely to do some literature-based research in order to understand the context you deal with and this could include consulting policy documents, government reports, surveys and other research studies.

Reflexivity

In ethnographic research, knowledge is created through social interaction (for example, in an interview). Meaning-making takes place through the encounter between researcher and researched. This means that in ethnography (and in the social sciences more generally) the connection between the researcher and the research setting is much closer than in the natural sciences. Both the researcher and the research subjects (the people being studied) are at the core of ethnographic research.

This is important because it means that, even in short-term ethnography, the relationship between the researcher and the researched will always be a close one and to a large extent relies on the researcher's personal involvement with her informants. The issue of proximity and distance is central to each ethnographic endeavour: as much as ethnography entails a process of coming closer to the research setting, it also requires the researcher to distance herself from the field experience. This is necessary in order to achieve a critical, theorising stance, which is at the heart of what academic enquiry aims to achieve.

It follows from the above that reflexivity is a central requirement of ethnography. Reflexivity means a turning on oneself, an awareness of how the product of research is affected by the personal and by the process of research (Davies 1999). For the researcher, to be reflexive means to scrutinise the conditions of how in the field researcher and researched come to understand each other and then agree on answers to questions the research has raised. This includes a discussion of the research methods chosen, but also an awareness of how subjectivity, individual experience and negotiations with informants figure in the process of interpretation. It is nowadays common practice among ethnographers to discuss these questions in the written products of their work.

The purpose of reflexivity, therefore, should not only be to disclose the process and conditions of knowing in the field, but to problematise these – by which we mean, to identify and analyse all the possible problems with the data collected and how it should be interpreted. As part of such a reflective stance, the researcher describes the process of research (including its difficulties and setbacks) and acknowledges gaps and challenges in her claims to authority. Accordingly, the researcher needs to question the grounds on which she arrives at her interpretations and to be constantly ready to check her own interpretations against those of the research subjects.

While a certain modesty and critical stance towards the results of one's own research seem now to be part of the common reflexive stance in ethnography, this does not mean that as ethnographers we have to descend into relativism. Even if, as Clifford (1986) has argued, ethnographic truths are always only part of the truth, we should not abandon a form of social science that serves intellectual, moral and political purposes. There are still enough grounds on which to argue for ethnographic data as being both valid and relevant, and this is certainly important when thinking about the role that research on literacy can play with regard to the practice and policy of adult literacy, numeracy and ESOL.

Ethnography as a research tool for practitioners

As mentioned earlier, one of the flagships of the New Literacy Studies is its interest in the role of literacy in everyday life. The NLS has moved researchers' interest away from educational contexts of literacy – the learning and teaching of reading and writing in classrooms – to the uses and meanings of literacy in everyday life. This is an important move. Among other things, it challenges us to show why studies of literacy in everyday life are relevant and interesting not only for researchers (interested in theoretical issues of the nature of literacy), but for teachers, curriculum developers, planners and policy-makers. In other words, the challenge is to bring everyday life back to the teaching context and to show how learning about people's uses of literacy (through ethnographies of literacy in different communities and contexts) can inform practitioners' and policy-makers' work.

The questions are simple. What can teachers gain from understanding how their learners use literacy and numeracy in their everyday lives? What can the government, what can colleges and other providers learn from the kind of studies Barton and Hamilton (and others) have produced? These are important issues for the social view of literacy, which at times has been accused of being an academy-based pastime of researchers who have little interest in the realities and struggles of teaching, planning and financing basic education and ESOL programmes for adults. The underlying concern is how can we apply the social view of literacy to the teaching of reading and writing. I have already begun to address this issue at the end of Chapter 3.

A central question is what role can ethnographic research play in, for example, informing teachers and planners about potential students' uses of literacy, the difficulties they face, the things they want to learn, and so on. In other words, what role could ethnographies of literacy play as a curriculum resource? A related question is whether ethnographic methods of the kinds discussed here can be used not only by 'professional' researchers but by teachers and students, and what they could learn from the process. I deal with both these questions in more detail in Chapter 8 of the book. In order to prepare the reader to understand the use of ethnographic research in literacy, below is a short research exercise for you to carry out while reading this book. It gives you a chance to try out some of the methods discussed here and to engage in a small-scale research study on an area of everyday literacy of your choice.

Research

Researching literacy practices of everyday life

The purpose of this activity is to conduct a small-scale study of literacy practices in everyday life. The idea is for you to select and focus on a particular situation or setting where literacy is used. Your task is to describe the literacy events that you observe in this context and, as far as possible, to identify the meanings of literacy in this particular setting.

Possible topics

You might research any area of literacy in everyday life, in workplaces or educational settings. You may decide to study your own family or friends, or an association or a club you belong to. You may want to focus on literacy practices in the home (from shopping lists to personal letters) or on public and bureaucratic literacies. Alternatively, you may be interested in particular workplaces, for example shops or surgeries, and the reading and writing involved in being a shop assistant or a receptionist.

These are examples of literacy practices outside educational institutions. There are many other such literacies, some related to specific cultural activities, others focused on particular technologies. Students at Lancaster University who took a course on literacy studies have researched the literacy practices of betting shops or dental surgeries. Others have considered how cultural outsiders, foreign students, migrant workers or refugees deal with the mainly English literacy practices that dominate written communication in day-to-day life. Another possibility is to look at the informal learning of new literacy practices that happens outside educational contexts. You could, for example, examine how people learn new electronic literacy practices, such as booking tickets on line, playing videogames or participating in online chatrooms. If you would like to focus on an educational setting, you may examine the literacy practices of an adult basic education class, of a university lecture or seminar, or of a particular vocational training course.

Here are some suggestions for investigations of literacy practices in and outside educational settings:

- Post Office
- Job search in the job centre
- Having a baby
- Planning a holiday abroad
- Seeking treatment for a common disease and/or being in hospital
- Reading and writing as part of an ante-natal class
- Literacy in a museum
- Children's literacy practices in school and at home
- The literacy practices of meetings

You can find further examples of research projects that students have undertaken on the Lancaster Literacy Research Centre website (www. literacy.lancs.ac.uk).

Whatever you choose, the purpose of your research will be to discover what is particular about the reading and writing involved in the activity or setting you have chosen.

Instructions

The goal of this activity is for you to look at reading and writing through the lens of the social theory of literacy.

Begin by identifying a domain or activity to focus your research on. This may be a specific physical space or a particular activity. Getting started may be difficult and you may wonder how to approach people in your chosen setting.

The Reading for this chapter may help you with your research: 'Methodology: tools for looking up close' is an extract from Judy Kalman's book *Writing on the Plaza* (1999, Cresskill, NJ: Hampton Press, pp. 28–33), in which she describes the research methods that she used for her study of scribing practices in Mexico City. Scribing is a common form of literacy mediation in many countries. Scribes – such as the ones Kalman interviewed, on a square in the centre of Mexico city – write and type letters for clients, fill out forms or print student essays. Part of their task may be to write a letter or to complete a form in a language the client is unfamiliar with. In the extract printed below, Kalman explains how she established contact with scribes in Mexico City and how her relationships with the scribes and their clients developed over the course of her research.

METHODOLOGY: TOOLS FOR LOOKING UP CLOSE

The recognition of literacy as a complex, multiple phenomenon has had a direct impact on research concerned with understanding reading and writing. Because of the highly situated nature of social practices, locating literacy in both broad social contexts and specific situations is fundamental to constructing an intricate view of written language use. Current qualitative research on literacy and literacy-related issues seeks to provide thick descriptions (Geertz, 1973) of reading and writing practices as they occur in different sociocultural settings and the meanings that these practices have for those involved in doing them (Barton, 1991; Bloome, 1993; Street, 1993c). The point of these case studies is not the "generation of decontextualized principles or generalizations at an abstract level but the derivation of principles and theoretical insights within particularity" (Street, 1993d, p. 86). The point of learning about how specific scribes and clients accomplished literacy, how they displayed it in actions and words and what literacy meant to them was to further understand first, what constitutes scribing as a particular form of mediated literacy practice and second, further our knowledge about literacy, what it is, and the many ways that it is achieved. Given this interest, I centered my attention on what the scribes did, what they said as they did it, and their reflections on reading and writing after their document was complete. The participants' talk (both the spontaneous comments that they made to each other as they worked and their opinions elicited through informal interviews) was an important source of information for this research.

This required looking at reading and writing in motion, inserted in the face-to-face interactions of scribes and clients where talk played an important role for organizing and carrying out written language activities. Central to this approach is the notion that practice, rather than a noun is a verb. The importance of treating cultural phenomena as activities lies in the need to recognize practices as "signifying processes – the active construction of meaning" – rather than as the static notion of fixed behaviors that tend to disguise issues of power and social change (Street, 1993b, p. 23). Practice is not a thing or an object, it is an action, there is only "*practicing*," done by someone situated in a (historical) time and place. It is accomplished through using a specific technology – computer or quill – and using specific techniques – pen and paper for drafting ideas, checking them off when typed into the computer. In this sense, skills cannot be abstracted from the situations in which they occur; for this reason this research focuses on literacy practices situated in the context of collaborative reading and writing as it occurs between scribes and their clients.

A working definition of *social practice* might be situated ways of operating in the world (de Certeau, 1984). Operating requires knowing what to do and knowing how to do it (Heller, 1984) and why. However, *know-how*, *know what*, and *know why* are not mechanically applied or branded on a set of circumstances. Social actors respond to a given situation, and in doing so they participate in the construction of the ongoing context. Gumperz (1990) defined context as a process, noting that expectations change about what is to be accomplished and are reformulated throughout speech exchanges. Responses, however, are not simple individual preferences or a matter of personalities. They are also socially construed, based on the assumptions and premises built through experience in the social world.

In order to get close to what literacy meant for the scribes and their clients and how they used reading and writing to act in the social world, I observed their activities, audiorecorded their talk, interviewed them, and collected written products. Data was gathered at the Plaza de Santo Domingo during three extended periods of residency in Mexico City that varied in length from 10 days to 4 weeks. During the time I was there, I "hung out" with the scribes, to borrow Agar's (1973) timely phrase. I spent an average of 5 hours daily at the square watching and recording the scribes and clients at work. I also kept a log based on "scratch notes" (Sanjek, 1991) written at the square. In between each planned visit to the research site, I transcribed all tapes.

As scribes and clients worked together, I tried to stand (or sit) in a place where I could listen to their talk and watch what they were writing and doing (referring to other documents, reading back something just written, correcting a mistake, etc.) without interfering with participants' view of each other. This varied because sometimes I would come upon a scribe and his client as they were beginning to work and so I could position myself behind or to the side of the scribe. Other times, however, I would be sitting and chatting with a scribe while he waited for a customer to come and the client would then choose his or her place accordingly. I generally offered my seat to approaching clients, men and women alike. The men never accepted it even though I made ceremonious efforts of insisting, and they would answer me with "*Siga ud. sentada*" ("Remain seated") or "*No, por favor señorita, siéntese ud.*" ("No, señorita. please be seated"). Most of the women that I observed at the square came accompanied by their sons, husbands, a male friend, or by other women. Only once did I see a scribe work with a woman by herself. Sometimes they would accept my seat, other times they would not.

Because many courses of study In Mexico, technical and academic alike, require a final product that comes under the general heading of *tesis* (thesis), the printing of them is a lucrative and common business. Those students who can afford it, print 50 to 100 copies of their *tesis* and give them to their teachers, friends, and relatives after graduation. Many of the printers in the fold-up stands in front of the scribes and the building behind them advertised in their front windows or on their signs "thesis printed here." Typing the final versions in preparation for printing is a common job for scribes. This made it quite easy to find scribes who were willing to let me watch and record them. I explained to the scribes that in Mexico I was a teacher and that I had gone abroad to study and was now doing my thesis. I asked for their permission and then their help for gathering information about the square, because where I studied no one knew about it. They were eager to assist me for the most part as long as I did not interfere with their work. As time went on, they asked me how my research was going, if I had enough (*data*), or if I had begun writing.

Gone are the days when participant observers pretend to be "objective" in their work (Rosaldo, 1989; Van Maanen, 1988). My closeness to the culture and my own assumptions about literacy played heavily into what was interesting to me, the questions that I asked, and the issues that I pursued. At first when I worked, I would try to stand to the side or behind the scribes as they wrote, but as we got to know each other better they would call me over, introduce me to their clients, and explain that I was a student doing work on my "thesis." Once the scribes knew me, they introduced me as their friend with varying degrees of endearment such as "my friend" ("*Es una amiga*," "*es mi amiguita Judith*"). The clients and I would shake hands. Because of my hosts and my shared notions of politeness I felt very much at home with their formal introductions. It also gave me an opportunity to comment on the tape recorder that I carried in my hand, which allowed clients to decline if they so wished.

Some clients took time away from the business that brought them to the square to question my story. They questioned me further about who I was, where I was from, and what I was doing. Sometimes the scribes helped me, saying things like, "she's writing about the Plaza and the work we do here" or "she's a student in the United States." One day, for example, Felipe (a scribe) and I were sitting and chatting about the square when an elderly woman, a retired teacher, approached the table and wanted Felipe to type up her document. He introduced us, and he told her that I was a student, that I was studying and doing my thesis. I further explained that in Mexico I, too, was a teacher. They settled on a price, and she (Maestra) began to explain what the document was about. Then she spoke to me directly:[4]

Maestra: Es un informe de una ¿ cómo se llama? Es de una escuela que le puso el doctor, el profesor que ya va acumplir 100 años . . . ¿ Cómo va a cumplir 100 años si ni la Independencia ha cumplido 100 años, o no? ¿ O ya cumplimos 100 años? Ud. como maestra . . .

Maestra: It's a report about a, what's it called? It's about a school that the doctor, the teacher started, and it's going to be 100 years old. How could it be 100 years old if the independence is not 100 years old yet? Or is it? Your being a teacher . . .

4 See transcription symbols in Appendix A. As Ochs (1979) pointed out, transcriptions are themselves the result of analysis, and I believe that the same goes for translation. The analysis was done directly with the data in Spanish, and I have provided English translations throughout. In translating, I tried to present language that most paralleled the tone and mode of the captured dialogues. I have included those transcription symbols that were readily transferable. Occasionally, a few words in Spanish that were too colloquial to be translated are sprinkled in the English section.

Kalman: Bueno, pues, la Independencia fue en 1810, entonces 1910 son cien=

Maestra: = ¿ 1910 qué?

Kalman: Fueron cien años=

Maestra: = 1910 empezó la Independencia

Kalman: No, 1810 fue la Independencia,

Maestra: A: sí.

Kalman: Y la Revolución fue más o menos de 1910 al 17

Maestra: Entonces fue el siglo pasado y luego empezó el siglo de 1900.

Kalman: Well, the Independence was in 1810, by 1910 that's 100 years

Maestra: 1910, what?

Kalman: It was 100 years

Maestra: 1910, the Independence started

Kalman: No, 1810 was the Independence,

Maestra: A: right.

Kalman: And the Revolution was in 1910 to 17, more or less.

Maestra: Then it was in the last century and then the 1900s started.

Because I had said that I was a teacher, too, the Maestra tested me on my knowledge of Mexican history. She asked me questions about landmark events, common to the national curriculum for primary school. She asked me several questions and when I gave her satisfactory answers, she "evaluated" me with an approving *sí*. Once I had passed the test and she was satisfied that my story was straight, she continued working with Felipe and let me stay and observe.

My stance as an observer changed over time and varied depending on who I was with and the way specific situations unfolded. When I returned to the square after each absence, I was warmly greeted by many people there, focal scribes as well as others. As I spent more time at the square, I became a familiar face to many of the scribes and printers. When one printer would try to sell me something, another would tell him that I was not a customer, I was a student. Or they would treat me to a soft drink, or offer me gum and candy. They shared their newspaper with me and one scribe wrote a poem for me as a Christmas present. I responded to people's kindness with my own anecdotes, stories, and pictures of my children. At different moments of the fieldwork my children and husband came to Santo Domingo to meet the scribes and other people on the square.

Once the scribes finished working on a document, I would follow the clients as they left the square. I interviewed them on the spot, because once they left it would have been impossible to talk to them. People went out of their way to help me, offering me copies of their documents, giving me their handwritten drafts, or letting me photocopy them. Only on two occasions did the clients seem reluctant or in a hurry. In both of those cases I shortened the interview. Most people chatted with me extensively, sometimes for as long as 1 hour. The interviews were open, but to facilitate them I used a small guide written on the top flap of my notebook. The questions centered around:

1 How they knew about the square, whether they came often, and whether they had previously worked with that particular scribe.
2 Whether they brought a handwritten draft with them, the history of that draft

(if they or someone else wrote it, why they drafted it first, why they wanted it typed).

3 Whether they had letterhead or asked for copies, and what the letters were for.

4 Whether there were discrepancies with the scribes, what the difference in opinion was and why they thought it was resolved in a certain way.

5 How many years of schooling they had and what their occupation was.

I interviewed each scribe several times in the course of the informal talks that we had. Business was slow many of the days that I spent at the square and my talks with the scribes often lasted for 1 hour before a client came or the scribe decided to get something to eat or go buy a newspaper. During these talks I wove questions about how they came to work at the square, what their job entailed and how they learned to do it, and about particular clients that I had observed them with, into our chatting about the weather, the smog, their families, and the history of the square (Briggs, 1986).

Once you have made contact with your research participants, there are several steps you can take:

1 Observe the visual environment: what texts can you find, what artefacts (e.g. computers, books, posters);

2 Describe the particular texts that are involved. If you can, collect examples of texts, or photocopy or photograph them;

3 Describe particular literacy events: observe the activities around these texts, focus on participants, settings, artefacts;

4 Interview people about their literacy activities: try to understand the meanings of literacy in this particular activity/setting.

In each step, you focus on particular aspects of the literacy practices you have chosen to study. In step 1 and 2, you describe the visual aspects of the literacy activity and focus on the texts that are involved. In step 3, you try to understand what is actually happening in a literacy event. In other words, you look at what people do with the texts you have identified as being central to the literacy event and what role the texts play in any action that follows. At the same time, you focus your attention on the people who engage in these activities. Who is involved in a particular literacy event? What roles do people take on: are they spectators or active participants? Are only certain people involved, for example, only men? What can you say about the relationships between participants?

Not all of the above will be directly observable from the literacy event. Depending on how far you wish to take your study, you may have to do some background research on the setting or activity you have chosen. If you can, as suggested in Step 4, you might want to interview participants about their literacy practices, trying to elicit the cultural knowledge and the social meanings associated with a particular literacy practice.

Analysis

Going from Step 1 to Step 4 gradually moves your research activities from describing the observable elements of a literacy event towards analysing the deeper meanings of a literacy practice. There are no strict recipes for how to do such research. However, whatever you choose, it is helpful to think of it as taking some distance from the event. Do not look at it from the perspective of an insider, who is a regular participant in the event. Look at the event with a stranger's eye. What is actually going on? And what do you need to know in order to understand what is going on? What you are doing is trying to make the familiar unfamiliar and to look at ordinary things from a new perspective. This may prove to be a very revealing experience, and hopefully it will help you to get an idea of the huge variety and the complexity of literacy practices of everyday life. Literacy has become such a regular ingredient of communication in our societies that we are rarely aware of the amount of literacy we are involved in every day.

In part, the purpose of this research activity is to help you identify some of these many everyday literacies. However, if possible, you should go further and try to uncover some of the patterns and the meanings that characterise these literacy events. You may, for example, note things such as the role of dominant institutions in your specific area, the relationships between different literacies, the significance of gender roles or networks of support, the ways in which texts try to prescribe particular meanings, differences between literacies in different languages, and so on. You may also want to think about the particular skills that are required when engaging with the literacy practices that you have chosen to study. You can also try to imagine what difficulties people may experience when dealing with these literacy practices.

Remember to look at detail and to use your 'stranger's eyes' when researching familiar literacy practices, that at first sight might seem banal and containing very little of interest for a social theory of literacy. If this is your impression, you will certainly be mistaken!

Additional reading

Barton, D. and Hamilton, M. (1998) *Local Literacies*, London: Routledge, chapter 4.

Davies, C.A. (1999) *Reflexive Ethnography*, London: Routledge, chapters 4 and 5 (on participant observation and interviews).

Part II

Implications for policy and practice

INTRODUCTION TO PART II

The first four chapters of this book focused on different theoretical perspectives on literacy and what these can tell us about the nature of reading and writing. Beginning with an introduction to the idea of literacy as a discourse (Chapter 1) – an ideologically framed position, which is grounded in particular assumptions about the nature of reading and writing and of language more generally – throughout chapters 2, 3 and 4, my primary aim was to present one particular understanding of literacy, that is the idea of reading and writing as social practice.

Beginning with Chapter 5, the book now moves towards examining more closely the nature of literacy and numeracy as pedagogical practice, and the various attempts that have been and are currently being made to help adults to improve their language, literacy and numeracy abilities. Chapter 5 provides an overview of the history of adult literacy, numeracy and ESOL policy in Britain. Chapter 6 deals with the current policy framework of adult LLN, focusing in particular on the new Skills for Life strategy that was introduced in 2001. In Chapter 7, I offer a critical analysis of the main policy discourses that underlie Skills for Life, looking at extracts from various policy documents and reports. Chapter 8, the final chapter, discusses the policy and practice implications of the social practice view of literacy, making suggestions how to use such an approach as a curriculum resource.

The social practices view of literacy, introduced in chapters 2–4, continues in Part II to serve as a guiding frame for my analysis, as it provides me with a lens through which to critically examine previous and current literacy policies and their ability to allow adults to acquire those literacy practices that are most meaningful and relevant to them. I shall also draw upon the various categories and discourses identified by Searle and Hamilton (see Chapter 1), as I will discuss for example to what extent a model of literacy as social control has been prominent in determining adult literacy policy in England.

Chapter 5

The history of adult literacy education in England

Introduction: a critical history of adult basic education

Since 1997, the Labour government has made the education of adults in England one of its priority policy areas and, as a result, concern for adult language, literacy and numeracy has taken a central role in the state's educational provision. However, adult education, and more particularly adult basic education (ABE, as it used to be called) has long been a neglected sector and it is worth tracing the history of ABE in England.

The critical account that I present concentrates in particular on the development of reading and writing instruction for adults. My purpose is to identify the struggles over the definitions and goals of literacy that underlie the development of literacy policy. I will relate these struggles to the different discourses about literacy that I introduced in Chapter 1. Different strands of provision have fed into the development of adult literacy policy. These were governed by different understandings of what adult literacy is supposed to achieve and how, institutionally, it should be organised. Such discourses about literacy have been conflicting. They developed within particular institutional settings and they have influenced adult basic education broadly in proportion to their human and financial resources. A critical history also means to try to understand developments in adult literacy policy not in isolation, but as they relate to and are shaped by, broader developments in society and in national and international policy.

The development of adult literacy in England will be described in three periods. The first major period begins with the discovery of adult 'illiteracy' as a major societal concern in the 1970s and the development of a first national effort for adult literacy education, the 'Right to Read' campaign. Beginning in the 1980s, the second period saw the gradual emergence of an increasingly formalised system of learning provision for adults. This change was accompanied by a re-definition of literacy itself, with an increasing focus on vocational goals for adult basic education. The third and current period began with the Moser Report in 1999. This report signalled the current government's new commitment to adult basic education, which culminated in the new national policy on language, literacy and numeracy, the Skills for Life programme. I will deal with the third, current period in chapters 6 and 7.

Historical roots: the Middle Ages and early modern Britain

Prior to the arrival of the Normans, literacy was exclusive to the clergy. The Normans insisted that land and property rights had to be legitimised by written documents (Clanchy 1979). With this they introduced the first secular uses of literacy. But despite these changes, throughout the Middle Ages and well into the 17th and 18th centuries, the use of literacy remained by and large limited to the clergy.

Between 1500 and 1800, educational institutions to teach literacy gradually emerged. These gained more importance from the mid-19th century onwards, at a time when efforts to institutionalise education became common all over Europe. Since education increasingly became a matter of concern for the churches and for the state, debates over its purpose and content began. These mirror some of the ideological views that we can still recognise in today's discussions about literacy and adult education (Street 1997). On one side of the debate, some educationists and theoretical thinkers made claims for the important role of literacy in developing rationality and abstract thought (and this resembles the Great Divide theories discussed in Chapter 2) and in supporting critical thinking skills and democracy. Similar claims were put forward by working-class activists in the 19th century (Vincent 2000; Mace 2002). These views were contradicted by politicians who were wary of the potential consequences of giving literacy to the poor and who wanted to see literacy education restricted to work discipline.

You may recognise in these debates some of the ideological strands that I discussed in Chapter 1: literacy for emancipation and literacy as control (Searle 1999). The distinction between reading and writing also first appeared at that time. Reading was seen as the more passive skill, and the teaching of reading was supported by the churches through their Sunday schools. Writing, however, was regarded as a potentially subversive skill and was much less encouraged.

Another theme familiar from current debates about literacy is the idea of 'illiteracy' as a disease or a lack that needs to be remedied (see Chapter 1 on metaphors for literacy). This idea can also be traced back to the 19th century, when liberal-minded members of the middle classes began to seek ways to teach literacy to the working classes. One such initiative was the Settlement Movement, which was founded in the 19th century, when university graduates from Oxford taught residents of poor areas of East London to read and write.

The discovery of 'illiteracy' and the 'Right to Read' campaign

Throughout the first half of the 20th century, there was little public concern about adult literacy. In part, this was because – with the introduction of universal compulsory primary education in the late 19th century and the extension of compulsory schooling into secondary education that followed in 1944 – it was assumed that everybody had learned to read and write. However, this was later found not to be the case.

Lack of literacy among adults was first recognised as a problem in the Second World War, when the army established Basic Education Centres for recruits. But this remained an isolated activity. From the 1950s onwards, UNESCO had begun its efforts to 'combat' illiteracy in developing countries. At that time the industrialised world still saw illiteracy as a problem belonging exclusively to the countries of the South. As a consequence, UNESCO's efforts found little resonance in the North. It was only in the 1970s that the UK and other countries began to see adult literacy as a potential matter of concern.

In England, government support for adult literacy began with the Right to Read campaign in the 1970s (Withnall 1994).The campaign, spearheaded by the BBC and the British Association of Settlements, was informed by a liberal view that emphasised rights and access to education for the entire population. The campaign was launched in 1973. In 1974, the government released one million pounds to support it, a relatively small amount compared to the annual investment in formal education. This reflected the state's view of the campaign as a temporary measure, the assumption being that a single, large-scale effort would be able to deal with what was seen as a minor problem.

As a result of these efforts, combined with the major publicity campaign set up by the BBC, adult literacy provision was quickly established in England (and Wales). Relying on the use of volunteers, it became part of adult education in every local education authority (LEA). A central government unit allocated funds to LEAs and voluntary bodies, and trained volunteers. This unit, the Adult Literacy Resource Agency (ALRA), was planned as a temporary structure. Yet, despite the huge success of the campaign in establishing literacy education all over the country, it soon became obvious that the problem of illiteracy could not be remedied so quickly and easily. In 1979, ALRA, which is today known as the Basic Skills Agency (BSA), was consolidated as a permanent structure.

The Right to Read campaign was primarily important in two respects. Firstly, it drew public attention to a problem that previously had not been recognised. Secondly, the campaign helped to develop what might be called important guiding principles of adult literacy education in Britain. The adult literacy teaching that developed in the 1970s was student-centred, and responsive to individual needs rather than to a pre-established curriculum. No regular or structured assessments existed. Since no materials for teaching adults had yet been developed, the production of reading materials with and by adult students themselves became an important strand of adult literacy work that continued into the 1980s. This, you could say, allowed teachers to build links with students' own literacy practices and it allowed students to write about their own concerns (amongst them those related to literacy and education). Emphasis was given to writing, and learning to write often included writing for publication (Gardener 1999–2000). While many activists and volunteers focused their efforts on confidence-building and developing student writing, others developed a more political viewpoint, influenced by Paulo Freire's work among others.

Despite the momentum generated by the campaign and the many people who were attracted to it, either as volunteer tutors or as students, the movement (if it can be called such) remained marginal compared to the efforts and funds invested in formal education. For the government, adult literacy remained a low priority. This was to change only in the late 1980s and early 1990s, when literacy began to be more closely associated with vocational skills and with the country's overall economic performance.

From liberal rights to economic justification: changing discourses of adult literacy in the 1980s and 1990s

Despite the initial grant given to the Right to Read campaign, funding for adult literacy provision was uneven and at best sketchy. Most adult literacy provision was financed by LEAs. ESOL received funding from the Home Office and as a consequence, literacy for speakers of other languages developed as a separate sector.

Overall, throughout the late 1970s and the 1980s, the sector grew steadily in terms of student numbers. Teaching and learning structures changed from the original one-to-one tutoring, which relied on unpaid volunteers, to small groups and open learning centres with part-time paid teachers. ALRA, later renamed ALU, then ALBSU and finally (in 1995) the BSA, fulfilled two important roles. It was influential as a body that controlled initial training and accreditation of tutors. Furthermore, it funded innovative development projects and produced a wide range of resource packs that were offered to teachers. Numeracy was taught as part of literacy instruction. This is reflected in the change from 'adult literacy', the term most commonly used in the beginning, to the broader concept of 'adult basic education' or 'adult basic skills'.

Throughout the 1980s, the government's growing concerns for the economy and the changing structures of employment led to increased debate over the need for new strategies to train and re-train employees. Gradually, economic concerns moved to the forefront of adult basic education policies. As a result, a vocational orientation was introduced into the adult literacy sector, which so far had been student-focused and broad-based. This was in line with the discourse of functional literacy that had become prominent in the 1960s and 1970s (see Chapter 1). With this major change in orientation, new goals for literacy and numeracy were established and new means to achieve these were defined. The change did not happen in a vacuum, but reflected broader societal and political changes associated with the crisis of welfare states, the rise of neo-liberal policies and changes in the workplace and in the structure of paid employment (see Hamilton 1998).

The Further and Higher Education Act of 1992

The turning point for adult basic education was the Further and Higher Education Act of 1992, as a result of which all funding for vocationally relevant adult education courses was channelled through further education colleges directly and no longer through LEAs. In practice, this meant a separation between vocational and non-vocational adult literacy programmes and very little money for non-vocational, community-orientated initiatives (Hamilton 1998). With the Act, the government clearly set its priorities for ABE: funding for adult literacy and numeracy was henceforth to be allocated to those programmes that would lead to recognised qualifications (such as Wordpower and Numberpower, introduced in 1989; see further, below). This new focus clearly reflects the shift from a definition of literacy that emphasised liberal rights towards a discourse of economic justification and vocationalism for literacy. At the same time, the new policy reflected a concern for illiteracy not only as an individual problem, but as a problem for the entire nation and in particular its economy.

As a result of the 1992 Act, adult basic education was integrated into the overall system of training and education, a move that gave the sector a potentially more secure status, backed up by more stable funding. Adult literacy and numeracy moved into the mainstream of continuing education. Provision shifted from community venues into colleges, where adult literacy and numeracy became part of foundation studies (Hamilton and Merrifield 2000). The government's growing interest in the sector also led to pressure for improved quality and uniformity of provision.

Although not a curriculum in the strict sense, the national Wordpower and Numberpower certificates, introduced in 1989, influenced the content of learning (Hamilton and Merrifield 2000). They made it more difficult for adult literacy and numeracy to continue as a flexible system that supported a broad variety of students' interests and addressed non-vocational learning demands, in particular because they tended to focus on literacy and numeracy as isolated skills. Students had to prove that they had acquired (what must be seen as) discrete and abstract competencies, not how they had improved their ability to deal with literacy and numeracy practices in real-life contexts.

This important distinction relates to the complex issue of how (and whether) changes in students' engagement with literacy practices can be measured. I will come back to the issue of testing and its effect on the curriculum in chapters 6 and 7, when I will discuss the current Skills for Life programme and its associated national tests and standards. In a sense, these new national tests continue a trend that first began with Wordpower and Numberpower: these accreditation systems left considerably less room to demonstrate the many personal gains, such as increased self-confidence, that students experienced.

In the eyes of many practitioners and researchers, the changes that affected the ABE sector in the late 1980s and 1990s resulted in a narrow discourse of adult literacy that eclipsed the original broad concerns of the sector, de-politicised its agenda, weakened its ties with communities and lost the student-centred approach that many regarded as the major strength of adult basic education in this country (Hamilton and Merrifield 2000). The focus on vocational skills narrowed the range of literacy practices that potentially could be included in the teaching. However, in positive terms the changes brought statutory rights to the sector, a broadening base of providers and increased professionalism, which many feel was needed.

What happened in England in the 1990s was paralleled in other industrialised countries. Key terms such as economic efficiency, global competitiveness and restructuring the economy moved to the forefront of political debate throughout the industrialised world. As a consequence, training and re-training of workers received increased attention. The belief in human resource development as an essential factor in determining a country's economic success increasingly shaped adult basic education policies in Europe, North America and Australia (see, for example, Sticht 2002; Castleton, Sanguinetti and Falk 2001). The resulting shift to a strong focus on vocational outcomes can be observed in many other countries. At the same time, other goals for adult education, related to personal development, social justice and democracy, have receded into the background.

'Alternative visions': examples of adult literacy and language initiatives from the 1980s and 1990s

Despite the above trends, community-orientated and student-centred adult basic education, which had developed from the 1970s onwards, still existed in the 1980s and 1990s. These initiatives showed the continuing influence of the liberal tradition of adult literacy on adult basic education in England. They presented 'alternative visions' (Hamilton 1998) to the dominant trends in adult basic education policy. One of these initiatives was the Yemeni Literacy Campaign in Sheffield (Gurnah 2000). The other 'alternative vision' – already mentioned earlier in this chapter – was student writing and publishing, which were a popular part of ABE in the 1970s and 1980s and still are today.

The Yemeni Literacy Campaign was set up in 1988 in response to demand from the Yemeni community. Despite having lived in England for more than a decade, 82 per cent of Yemeni men interviewed in Sheffield in 1987 were not literate in English, and 67 per cent of the interviewed women reported having very low literacy skills in English. The campaign was organised by Sheffield's Multi-cultural Education Service in partnership with the Yemeni community and a local university that trained literacy assistants. These assistants were young, unemployed people from the community. While they recruited and taught learners, they themselves took part in a one-year access course at the university. The idea was that, on successful completion of their course, the literacy assistants could take up university studies.

The structure and organisation of the campaign was the result of in-depth consultation with the Yemeni community. Among the key principles identified and put into practice was a management team drawn from the community, which ensured that the community took the lead in implementing the campaign. A spirit of mutual learning and exchange of experiences governed the teaching. The language resources of each learner were brought into the classroom and this meant that a bilingual or dual-language approach was developed. It also meant that bridges were built with the learners' own everyday literacy practices and their own linguistic resources. This is exceptional, as central government funding for ESOL did not include provision for native language or bilingual programmes. The need for minority-language speakers to continue to use and develop their own language had rarely been recognised and it was (and still is) not seen as part of the state's responsibility to cater for such needs. Despite the lack of central government support for bilingual programmes, a small number of initiatives similar to the Yemeni campaign existed in the 1980s and 1990s, involving among others speakers of Caribbean languages (see Morris and Nwenmely 1994; Schwab 1994).

The interest in student writing, which first emerged during the Right to Read campaign, continued throughout the 1970s and 1980s (for examples of student writing initiatives, see Mace 1995). Student writing and publishing played an important role in adult language, literacy and numeracy provision. An example is *Write First Time*, a newspaper–magazine of writing by adult learners from across the country, published between 1975 and 1985. Sue Gardener (1999–2000), who was involved in the production of *Write First Time*, recalls the potentially political nature of student writing and the influence of Paulo Freire's ideas on their work. In the 1980s this met with less and less approval from the government, which tried to push adult basic education provision towards a greater emphasis on vocational skills. A further example of the more radical and democratic tradition of adult basic education that was strong in the 1980s and 1990s was the Pecket Well residential college for adults. Founded in 1992, near Halifax in the north of England, Pecket Well runs residential courses by and for adult students and it is strongly grounded in a tradition of democratic learning (Pecket Well College 1994; Hamilton 1998). Part of the tradition of Pecket Well is its emphasis on student writing and the publication of students' texts.

In the next two chapters, I will turn to more recent developments in adult language, literacy and numeracy policy in England.

Reading

Have a look at the extracts from *A Right to Read*. The British Association of Settlements (BAS) produced this document to alert the public and the government to what the BAS perceived as the problem of illiteracy in the country and to suggest ways for the government to set up a system of literacy education for adults.

Part 1 of *A Right to Read* aims to define the problem. It includes a chapter on the 'readability' of everyday documents such as leaflets and newspapers, and accounts of the lives of people who have difficulties with reading and writing. Part 2 suggests a course of action to tackle the problem.

Text printed below includes:

- extracts from Part 1, which deal with the number of people in England and Wales suspected to be 'illiterate' and with the issue of 'readability' of texts;
- two portraits of people with reading and writing difficulties.

The selected extracts are particularly interesting for three reasons: the mixture of discourses about literacy they present, the way they describe the so-called illiterates, and the various voices that are present and are given more or less authority in different parts of the texts (Pitt 2004). When I talk about discourses here, I mean discourses in the sense defined in Chapter 1 (particular ways of representing aspects of the world) and I have in mind the various discourses about literacy that Hamilton and Searle have suggested (see Chapter 1, Readings 1 and 2).

A Right to Read, British Association of Settlements: London, 1974, pp. 4–13

There are at least two million functionally illiterate adults in England and Wales.

That means that something like six per cent of the adult population is either unable to read or write at all or has a literacy level below that which you might expect to find in a nine-year-old child.

Two million people who are at a chronic disadvantage in their work and their leisure.

Two million people effectively isolated from many of the benefits, pleasures and experiences that the rest of us take for granted: people who cannot participate fully in our predominantly literate society.

This figure is not based on direct research because none is available; there has never been a national survey. It is based on the best related evidence, and on the firm opinions of acknowledged experts in the field.

BAS has accepted this figure of two million with caution, and only after critically examining all the available evidence. First we tried to arrive at the lowest figure the statistics might imply.

THE LOW FIGURE

The 1971 Census returns indicate that there are around 36,800,000 men and women over the age of eighteen in England and Wales.

The National Foundation for Educational Research has made six surveys of reading ability since 1948. The results are summarised in 'The Trend of Reading Standards' (Slough: NFER, 1972).

A figure rather more modest than the average of all these results indicates that at least 0.5 per cent of the adult population is completely illiterate, and at least 2.5 per cent is semi-literate.

These figures suggest at least a million adults with a reading age lower than that of the average nine-year-old child.

There are a number of reasons why this line of inquiry almost certainly results in a gross underestimate of the numbers of illiterate adults, even within its own terms:

1. It only takes into account people of eighteen and over, ignoring the sixteen- and seventeen-year-olds, who are also part of the adult population.
2. Literacy levels have improved since 1948, when the first study was undertaken, so that it is obviously an underestimate to apply its ratios to those who were educated before the war and therefore not included in the studies.
3. We have applied the same ratios to Wales as to England, though Welsh children at eleven and fifteen have been found to be less literate than their English contemporaries.
4. Special schools were not included in the surveys. They are bound to contain a relatively high proportion of the worst readers for their age.

THE REALISTIC FIGURE

Two authorities have persuaded us to accept that a more realistic figure for functionally illiterate adults is two million at least.

At the BAS conference, 'Status: Illiterate', held in London on 7th November 1973, Dr. Joyce Morris, the principal speaker, gave two reasons for supporting a higher figure:

> That the results of the most recent NFER Survey indicated that 'reading standards are not better today than they were a decade ago'. This statement

suggests that as many as seven to ten per cent of teenagers leaving school have a very poor reading ability. That implies a figure of two million at least in the adult population;

A figure of one million suggests that reading standards in the United States, which have been far more thoroughly researched than they have in this country, are five times lower than our own. This seems highly improbable. An estimate of two million functionally illiterate adults in this country still allows the Americans more than twice the illiteracy rate that we suffer from.

Our second authority is Peter Clyne in his 'The Disadvantaged Adult: Educational and Social Needs of Minority Groups' (London: Longman, 1973). He believes that two million English and Welsh adults are functionally illiterate.

BAS now accepts this figure as a basis for discussion and reform. And every single expert and educationalist we have questioned on the matter accepts it too.

It is a figure we should find quite horrifying. A figure that must shake our confidence in the basic thoroughness of our education process.

A further pointer towards an even higher figure, if we are to talk realistically about functional literacy, is that UNESCO draws the line not at nine-year-old reading levels as the English and Welsh research does, but at thirteen-year-old reading levels. How many more do we add if we accept that extra four-year gap?

FUNCTIONAL LITERACY

We use the term 'functionally literate' because we cannot simply be concerned about the people who can read or write nothing at all. There are probably five times as many who can read a little but whose attainment is so low that in practical terms it is more or less useless to them. They are functionally illiterate.

The United States National Reading Center provides a good working definition of functional literacy:

'A person is functionally literate when he has command of reading skills that permit him to go about his daily activities successfully on the job, or to move about society normally with comprehension of the usual printed expressions and messages he encounters.' Mimeographed (Washington NRC, 1971).

The best way to illustrate the practical effects of functional illiteracy is to show how many familiar and commonplace pieces of writing are beyond the reach of the person with a reading age of less than thirteen years.

We present a series of examples, but with the following reservation: there are a number of ways of measuring the readability of a piece of writing and none of them are entirely accurate, they should be taken simply as a useful and generally reliable guide.

For the purposes of our research we have elected to use a method employed by the US Army to test the readability of its training manuals. It is called FORCAST, and has the virtue of being the simplest test we have so far encountered. It is based on analysing the number of monosyllabic words in any passage of exactly 150 words (it cannot be used on shorter passages). The method is fully explained on pp. 339–369 of 'Literacy Discussion Vol. IV No. 3 Sept. 1973' (International Institute for Adult Literacy Methods. UNESCO).

Some of the results of these exercises surprised us, as they will probably surprise the reader. Many commonplace things are just not as simple as perhaps their producers think they are.

One thing must be clear, though: this is in no sense a plea for simplification. There may be cases where that is appropriate, but our concern is for a raising of the number of literate people, not the lowering of readability levels. Nor is it a criticism of the commercial products we have looked at.

SOME EXAMPLES OF READABILITY

We took the label off a bottle of household disinfectant. We looked at two separate parts of the label, one of them the warning to keep the product out of the reach of children, and also the instructions in case some of the disinfectant should accidentally be swallowed.

In both the samples we took, the reading age required to understand them was just over sixteen years.

EXTRA GRIP – STRONGEST AGAINST DIRT & GERMS
THE THICKER BLEACH CLEANSER

New ▇▇▇ is thicker so it clings more effectively to slippery surfaces. Cleans thoroughly above the waterline as well as below. ▇▇▇ is the sure answer to dirt and germ problems. Sure because ▇▇▇ contains a specially processed form of Sodium Hypochlorite, the strongest known germ killer for home use. Ideal for:–

LAVATORIES
Pour undiluted ▇▇▇ round the bowl every night to kill all germs and remove stains – even round the bend.

SINKS
1/2 eggcup ▇▇▇ to washing-up bowl of water. Wipe down sinks and working surfaces. Rinse.

WASTEPIPES
Pour undiluted ▇▇▇ down sink wastepipe. Leave 2 to 3 minutes then rinse thoroughly.

OUTSIDE DRAINS
Pour undiluted ▇▇▇ down drains. This will disinfect and destroy the waste matter which causes unpleasant smells.

BLEACHING
Cold bleach: 1 eggcup ▇▇▇ per gallon of water. Steep 45 minutes. Use half strength solution if steeping overnight.

Stain removal: 1 eggcup ▇▇▇ per gallon of cold water. Soak 5–15 minutes. This will remove most ordinary stains.

Do not use undiluted ▇▇▇ on clothes. Always mix with water first and rinse well after use. ▇▇▇ should not be used for silk, wool, coloureds, crease-resistant, drip-dry, embossed or piqué fabrics unless approved by manufacturer.

Do not use ▇▇▇ for cleaning baths.

CAUTION
KEEP OUT OF REACH OF CHILDREN

Wash off accidental splashes of undiluted ▇▇▇ promptly. If in the eyes or on the skin wash immediately in water. If swallowed, drink plenty of milk (or water) and then seek medical advice.

Do not use ▇▇▇ with other lavatory cleansers.

Store in a cool place – keep upright.

Do not over-tighten cap.

Then we looked at a selection of newspaper stories. To be accurate as possible we selected a single story and analysed several newspapers' treatment of it to see how the readability varied from paper to paper.

In this case we selected The Times, The Guardian, the Daily Express. The Sun and the Daily Mirror.

SCRAP INDUSTRIAL ACT, SAYS TOP BOSS

By KEITH MASON

THE Industrial Relations Act must be repealed.

Top boss Mr Campbell Adamson told

this to an industrial conference yesterday. The next Government must do it, he said, but there must be something else to replace it first.

Mr Adamson said that if unions and employers could agree on a new Act they should be given a chance to start again "so that every relationship at national level is not sullied by this Act.

"I would like to see the next Government saying right from the beginning: We will repeal the Act, but we will repeal it only when we have some joint agreement that would succeed it," he said.

Hatred

It was the most outspoken admission yet from Britain's bosses that the Act has been a failure.

The Labour Party have promised to repeal the Act immediately, and seek a new deal with the unions and employers if they are returned to power.

The Tories have so far offered only to amend the

Act in consultation with unions and employers.

Mr Adamson, director-general of the Confederation of British Industry, told the Industrial Society conference in London that the Act had been surrounded by hatred.

There were six major challenges facing British industry and management in 1974.

He listed them as the energy situation, the balance of payments, recovery from the miners' strike, increasing productivity and appreciating a more analytical and educated work force.

The sixth challenge was to take the previous five in the European context.

The Sun

The simplest treatment was in The Sun, as expected, though in this case even that required a reading age of just over fourteen years by the FORCAST test. A year above the functional literacy level proposed by UNESCO.

The interesting result was that all the other papers whose stories were tested had written with exactly the same degree of readability as each other. Their stories

CBI chief calls for unions Act repeal

By Raymond Perman
Labour Staff

Mr Campbell Adamson, director-general of the Confederation of British Industry, called yesterday for the repeal of the Industrial Relations Act, which he said had sullied every relationship between employers and unions at national level.

His remarks went much farther than previous CBI policy on the Act, which was broadly as outlined in the Conservative Party election manifesto; that it should be amended but not repealed.

His statement, to a conference of Labour managers organized by the Industrial Society will provide political ammunition for the Labour Party, which is committed to repealing the Act.

Mr Adamson said: "I should like to see the next government repeal the Act so that we can get proper agreement on what should replace it." He thought the unions would then be willing to discuss the place of law in industrial relations.

"We should go farther than amendment. It is so surrounded by hatred that we must have a more honest try at another Act. I have a feeling that the trade unions, faced with this sort of situation, would be quite ready to talk about it. This would give us a chance to start from a position where every relationship at a national level was not sullied by this Act."

He added that some parts of the Act were useful. It had made employers think more deeply about their relationships with employees.

Earlier, Mr Adamson said that, if the miners' strike ended by mid-March, industry could recover quite quickly. But it would still have to face production control difficulties in the face of continuing shortages of raw materials, lack of confidence in British industry abroad, the effects of the crisis on the investment programme and the need to keep prices low.

The Times

about Mr. Campbell Adamson's statement all required a reading age of nearly sixteen and a half years.

There was not the slightest difference in the reading ability required to understand The Times and the Mirror stories, though the FORCAST test can take no account of the effect of presentation and layout.

Analysis of other stories on different topics seemed to confirm these examples as fairly typical.

For instance, though we did find a Mirror leading article that required a reading age of no more than fourteen, a football story on the sports page of the same issue required a reading age of sixteen and a half.

A story in The Sun, this time about a kidney transplant, required a reading age of more than sixteen.

Then we looked at the instructions on the back of a pastry mix packet. They were among the simplest items we analysed, but still required a reading age of just over fourteen years before they could be applied.

short pastry mix

Mixing Instructions
Empty pastry mix into a bowl crushing any lumps with a fork. Sprinkle on 2 fl. oz. (4 dessertspoons) cold water for the 12 oz packet or 1½ fl. oz. (3 dessertspoons) cold water for the 8 oz packet and mix with a fork. Press into a ball with the fingers.

Serving Suggestion – Steak & Kidney Pie

Meat Filling: 1¼ lb braising or stewing beef, ¼ lb kidneys, 1 tablespoon flour, 1 level teaspoon salt, ¼ level teaspoon pepper, 1 small onion, ½ pint stock (made from beef stock cube)

Step 1 Trim and cut meat into cubes. Remove skin from kidneys and chop into pieces. Toss meat and kidneys in the flour, salt and pepper mixed. Place in casserole dish with the onion and pour on boiling beef stock. Cover with lid and cook in oven for 2½–3 hours or until the meat is tender at 275°F–Mark 1. Transfer the meat into a 1½ pint pie dish with some of the gravy. Arrange the meat slightly domed to prevent pastry from falling in whilst cooking. Leave until the meat is cold.

Step 2 Preheat the oven to 400°F – Mark 6. Mix the contents of this packet as per mixing instructions above. Turn pastry out onto lightly floured board and knead until smooth; roll out 1 inch larger than the pie dish. Cut off a strip all round 1 inch wide and press this into dampened rim of pie dish, then brush with cold water.

Step 3 Lift rest of pastry and place it over pie dish. Press down well and trim edge. Flute the edge at 1 inch intervals with back of a knife. Make a hole in pie centre to allow steam to escape.

Step 4 Roll out pastry trimmings and cut into leaves; decorate the centre and brush pastry with beaten egg. Bake in centre of oven for 20–25 minutes until golden brown. Reheat remainder of gravy to serve with pie.

Leaflet FIS 1, issued by the Department of Health and Social Security: Family Income Supplement.

The readability of this leaflet varied a good deal from paragraph to paragraph. One section required a reading age of fourteen years, another a reading age of nearly fourteen and a half. But the most important part of the leaflet, dealing with how to make a claim, required a reading age of just over seventeen years.

Other benefits you will be entitled to
Prescribed amounts

Number of children in your family	Levels of income below which you qualify	Maximum supplement payable
1	£21.50	£5
2	24.00	5
3	26.50	6
4	29.00	6
5	31.50	6
6	34.00	6

For each additional child the level in the second column is increased by £2.50

If you get FIS you will also be entitled to:–

- **Free prescriptions, free dental treatment and glasses** under the National Health Service
- **Free milk and vitamins** – for expectant mothers and children under school age.
- **Free school meals** – for children at school.
- **Refund of fares** for members of your family attending hospital for treatment.
- **New legal aid** – subject to certain capital limits.

Further information about these benefits will be given when your supplement is paid.

How to claim
Just complete the claim form, tear it off and send it to the Department of Health and Social Security, Family Income Supplements, Norcross, Blackpool FY5 3TD. You can get a franked addressed envelope at Post Offices or local Social Security offices.

Your claim will normally be decided from the information you give on your claim form and there should be no need for individual interviews. Any information you give will be treated as confidential. We will need to know your earnings, and it will help if you can send pay slips with your claim form for the last four weeks before the date you claim; if you are monthly paid you should send two monthly pay slips. Don't delay sending in your claim because you haven't enough pay slips. If necessary, we will send you a certificate for your employer to complete. If you are self-employed you should send your latest profit and loss account. Don't delay sending in your claim if this is not available.

Family Income Supplement
Family Income Supplement (FIS) is a benefit of up to £5 a week for families with one or two children and up to £6 a week for larger families. You can claim if you are living in England, Scotland or Wales and

- your total family income is below a certain level *and*
- you have at least one child in your family, *and*
- you are in full-time work.

In the case of a couple it must be the man who is in full-time work.

Income*
The level of income below which you can get FIS is called the 'prescribed amount'. The level depends on the number of children in your family, and is the same if there is only one parent in the family. See the table on page 3. You can claim the supplement if your total income, including gross earnings (which includes basic pay, regular overtime and/or bonuses), family allowances and wife's earnings is below this level; the income of children is disregarded. Some items of other income are also disregarded, eg the first £2 of a war disablement pension and the whole of any attendance allowance.

Children in the Family
Anyone, including single people, whose family includes at least one dependant child can claim. All children under 16, and those over 16 who are still undergoing secondary education, are included in your family if they live with you.

Full-time work
You must be, and must normally be, in full-time work, and in the case of a couple this means the man. 'Full-time work' means 30 or more hours a week. This applies to both employed and self-employed people.

The amount you get
The supplement you get is one half of the amount by which your family's total income falls below the prescribed amount. If the result is 10p or less, no supplement is paid. Odd amounts are rounded up to the next 10p above, and the minimum amount payable is 20p a week. The maximum payment is £5 for families with one or two children and £6 for larger families. Some examples of how the supplement is worked out are shown on page 4. Usually the supplement is awarded for 52 weeks and is not affected if your circumstances change during that time.

*Increased rates from 2 October 1973 subject to approval of Regulations by Parliament.

Leaflet PC 11, issued by the Department of Health and Social Security: Free Prescriptions.

This was by far the least accessible of the leaflets we analysed.

Analysed at three separate points, the reading ages FORCAST indicated were, in the first one, well over seventeen years, in the second, fifteen and a half years, and in the third, sixteen and a half years.

---

certificate because of your income, you will be able to get free prescriptions for up to 12 months. If you have already paid the prescription charge, attach the chemist's receipt form EC57 to the claim form. If you intend to claim a refund you must get this receipt form when you pay the charge. If you are unable to pay for the prescription, take the prescription form to your local Social Security Office, where you will be given an exemption certificate if you are entitled to it.

How you qualify on grounds of income

The way in which your entitlement is worked out for free prescriptions or refund of charges is explained on pages 4 and 5. Some examples of the income limits up to which people may qualify for free prescriptions or refund of charges are given below. *The examples, which relate to people at work, are a general guide only.* The income limits are gross incomes i.e. before the deduction of income tax and national insurance contributions. The limits also include the amounts shown for rent and rates, and fares to work. If your rent and rates or expenses connected with your work, e.g. fares, are higher or lower than those shown, then the limits would also be higher or lower.

If you are not working, then the income limits would be lower than the gross limits shown, and you should look at the fuller explanation on pages 4 and 5 of how entitlement is calculated.

Income guide for people at work

Size of family	Estimated rent and rates actually paid *after* deducting any rebates	Estimated employment expenses (e.g. bus or train fares)	Gross income limits i.e. gross earnings including family allowance where applicable but *before* deducting tax and NI contributions.
Single householder	£2.80	60p	£15.40
Married couple	£2.80	60p	£20.75
with child aged 4	£3.10	60p	£22.60
with 2 children aged 4 and 8	£3.45	60p	£25.55
with 3 children aged 4, 8 and 11	£3.45	60p	£28.55
with 4 children aged 4, 8, 11 and 16	£4.45	60p	£34.95
with 5 children aged 4, 8, 11, 14 and 16	£4.45	60p	£39.05

PEOPLE AND READING

This kind of analysis only begins to mean something when it is related to individuals and the specific difficulties.

Illiterate adults can be grouped according to their reading levels as follows:

complete beginners who cannot read or write anything beyond a few words of two or three letters and perhaps their own names and addresses;

intermediates whose basic reading ability is that of the average seven-to-nine-year-old, and who need help to master the skills of phonic analysis, fluency and basic spelling;

poor spellers who can read quite fluently but spell only the simplest words.

It is a common misconception that all people with chronic reading problems are at least educationally sub-normal, if not mentally defective.

But none of the statistics we have quoted in this report have included adults from either of those categories, though, of course, they suffer from a high level of illiteracy.

The statistics we have made use of refer to adults whose disability is illiteracy, which may stem from a variety of causes but cannot be explained away by mental incapacity.

Most of them are extremely ashamed of their handicap. Many develop the most elaborate deceptions to conceal their inability to read. Some go as far as carrying pairs of broken glasses in their pockets as an excuse for not being able to read, others avoid writing by wearing permanent bandages on their hands.

Many turn concealment into a way of life, and only a tiny minority seem to realise that there are classes which might be able to help them.

Very few dare expose themselves to the possibility of ridicule by coming forward and asking for help.

When they do come forward it is often because they fear that someone is about to find them out anyway. Perhaps a son or daughter is constantly pestering to be read to, or for help with homework.

Perhaps an employer is encouraging a man or woman to go for promotion which will mean filling in an application form, going on a training course, or even just making a few notes from time to time.

Only the most determined, or the luckiest find help at the moment. This is clear from the experiences of the illiterate adults we interviewed for this report, all of whom are now receiving, or are about to receive help.

ILLITERATE ADULTS

Who are the illiterate adults? They are a wide variety of men and women doing all sorts of different jobs, suffering from their inability to read in different ways.

Here are six of them. We have respected their general wish for anonymity and altered their Christian and surnames.

Brian Marks is twenty-five. He's a London motor fitter and has been married for four years. He is quite articulate but can neither read nor write.

'If someone asks me to spell something', he explains, 'I can get the first letters and sometimes the end, but not the middle.

'If I pick a paper up there are things I've seen lots of times and I have no problem. But if it's different I'm beaten. If I see a word like "police" or "ambulance" I know what it is because I've seen it so many times before. But if somebody just asked me to spell it I couldn't. It doesn't really matter about the length either, some of the smallest words can beat me.

'I just look at the front of the paper and maybe the TV pages. But it's only in the last two years that I've really bothered.

'But now we're buying a house and I've found it very awkward.

'Sometimes letters come and they're important, and I come home for lunch and my wife doesn't, so I can't read them. I just have to wait for her to come home.'

As a motor fitter Brian earns about £33 a week. He's a skilled man, but his reading difficulties have prevented him changing to a better job and could well have prevented him getting as far as he has.

'It was awkward at first. We had time sheets to fill in every day. When the fitter I was working with first found out he hit the roof. Then he did them for me.

'Now I'm a fitter I have to do them myself. But where I work there are quite a few like me, and one word that one of us doesn't know another will. And you use the same words every day and get to know them.

'There was a job vacant for a receptionist/tester, but I couldn't go for that. It would have meant about another £15 a week.

'And the people who make the automatic gearboxes we fit have offered me a job as a representative. But at the moment I just couldn't do that.' Brian puts his illiteracy down to bad school attendance. He blames it on his mother who, he says, was always keeping him at home to look after her in imaginary illnesses.

'I kept it from my wife', he says, 'more or less until we got married. She gradually got to know over quite a long period.

'The main thing is that if we went out in the car I couldn't read the map and had to give it to her. That's a giveaway.

'Before I met her I always used to go to Herne Bay year after year for my holidays, simply because I knew how to get there.

'And my driving test itself. That was a hard one. I didn't pass until third time. I was really frightened about the Highway Code.

'Another bad one was when Dad died. I had everything to do. Especially the Town Hall – I had to fill in the Death Certificate. I was in a right state over that. Luckily one of my aunts came with me.

'Even getting the colour TV, when we rented that I had to wait for my wife to do it. And the log book and insurance for the car are in her name.'

Brian has taken the step of asking for help and is waiting to start work with a tutor in an independent literacy scheme. He says he comes across plenty of other people who can't read either. 'For a start there's my two brothers. The best man at my wedding. A couple of youngsters at work, and a couple of the older ones too.'

Tony Dawes is a seventeen-year-old interior and exterior decorator in Birmingham.

'When I left school I was fifteen', he says. 'I couldn't read at all then. Well, there'd be bits here and there, just the odd word I could pick out.

'I could write my name. I couldn't write my address at all.

'At school they put me on those tape recording machines for about half an hour a day. You were left on your own in a corner of the room with a tape recorder and a book, and nobody helped you.

'You just tried to work out what it was and then play it back to yourself. If it didn't sound right you'd read it again. Then the teacher listened to it. You got fed up of it because you didn't know what you were reading.'

Tony has now been receiving individual tuition one night a week for four months. 'I think there's been a great improvement since I started. I've got some faith now and I can pick up a paper and read a lot better than I did. 'I've got the confidence now. I can see what's on TV, and I can fill my timesheet in at work. I used to have to take it home to my parents.

'Nobody knows about it at work now. But I'm not ashamed of it. I used to be, but I'm not now. I stopped being ashamed of it as soon as I realised I wasn't the only one.

'I tell my girlfriends about it, and I haven't really got that many mates, just a few. Some of them laugh at me, and some of them just say, "So what?"'

Tony found help through the Samaritans: 'I got fed up because I couldn't fill in my tax forms or anything.

'If I went on holiday I couldn't write to my girlfriends. And if I got letters my parents had to read them for me. Now I can read them for myself.'

Reflection

1. Have a look at pages 4–11 of the document, as shown on pp. 84–93.

   - What discourses about literacy can you find? Are these the same as in the Foreword?
   - Reading through the text carefully, whose voices are most strongly represented? Those of the illiterates themselves? Others, perhaps 'expert' voices? Whose positions are cited as authoritative?

The document devotes a full section to the discussion of 'readability' and 'reading levels' and goes to great lengths to show that many of the kind of texts we encounter every day require a high reading age. What is missing from this discussion? Try to think from a perspective of literacy as a social practice and try to put yourself in the position of those who deal with such texts.

   Now read the portraits of 'illiterates' on pages 12–13, as shown on pp. 94 and 95. How are people with reading and writing difficulties described? To what extent do these portraits depict a different view of 'illiteracy' from the previous pages of the booklet?

Additional reading

Gardener, S. (1999–2000) 'Student writing in the 70's and 80's: What we did, why, what happened', *RaPAL Bulletin* 40: 8–12.

Hamilton, M. (1998) 'Keeping alternative visions alive', *RaPAL Bulletin* 36.

Chapter 6

The current context of adult language, literacy and numeracy policy in England

What this chapter is about

Since 2001, the system of adult language, literacy and numeracy (LLN) provision in England has undergone major changes, prompted by the Labour government's drive towards providing better education and training facilities for the entire population. In this chapter, I examine in depth the current policies for adult language, literacy, and numeracy in England. The aim of this chapter is to develop a critical understanding of these policies, using as a starting point the social view of literacy.

My focus over the next pages is on the Skills for Life strategy that was launched in England in 2001. I ask what concept of literacy underpins this policy and I compare it with previous approaches to the teaching of literacy, numeracy and ESOL. I also briefly look at policy developments in the other countries of the UK and compare these with the approach to adult LLN in England. I begin by putting the new policy into its historical context, as discussed in the previous chapter.

The development of adult language, literacy and numeracy provision since the 1960s can be described in three distinct periods (see Chapter 5). The first period centred around the Right to Read campaign and the discovery of adult illiteracy as a major social concern in the 1970s. Throughout the second period, provision for adult language, literacy and numeracy gradually became more institutionalised and formalised, and increasingly focused on work-related aspects of literacy and numeracy. The third and current period began with the publication of the Moser Report (see below) in 1999. On the whole, the third period presents a continuation of the ideologies and aims that underpinned the second period: a focus on economic goals and further moves to institutionalise and professionalise the adult basic education sector. What is distinct about the current period is the strong commitment by the government to adult basic education as part of a wider social policy and its efforts to standardise and centralise the overall system of provision.

Skills for Life: a new national strategy for improving literacy, language and numeracy skills

In 1998, the Labour government commissioned a major review of adult basic education. The study led to the publication of *A Fresh Start* by Sir Claus Moser, in 1999. The Moser Report laid the grounds for a new direction in adult basic education that led to the Skills for Life strategy. It suggested a more centralised system of provision with a core national curriculum, national qualifications and national tests.

The government launched Skills for Life, its new national strategy for improving adult literacy and numeracy in England, on 1 March 2001. Its aim was to give 'all adults in England the opportunity to acquire the skills for active participation in the twenty-first century society and to engage their energy and commitment' (David Blunkett, *Skills for Life*, Executive summary, DfEE 2001a: 2).

In order to achieve this, in November 2002 the government announced that it would spend £1.6 billion across government to support the development of literacy, language and numeracy provision for adults. The initial aim was to have improved the literacy and numeracy skills of 750,000 adults by July 2004, a target later deferred to the autumn of 2004. In order to make this possible, 'over 2 million flexible learning opportunities' were to be provided (DfEE 2001a: 9). The target for 2007 is to have doubled the number of those who have significantly improved their skills, which would bring the total number of all those who benefited from the policy to 1.5 million adults. The government has identified the following priority groups: unemployed people and others who receive benefits, prisoners, public-sector employees, those who are employed but have low skills, homeless people, refugees and asylum-seekers, as well as others whose first language is not English.

How the new system works

A new unit, the Adult Basic Skills Strategy Unit (ABSSU) at the Department for Education and Skills (DfES, previously the Department for Education and Employment) was set up to oversee implementation of the strategy. New national curricula for literacy and numeracy have been in use since September 2001, the new ESOL curriculum was launched in February 2003 and a Pre-Entry Curriculum Framework (for those with learning difficulties and disabilities who have not yet reached Entry 1 in the Adult Literacy and Numeracy Core Curricula; see below) was also developed. New national literacy and numeracy tests were developed and new adult literacy and numeracy standards for all learning programmes were established. 'Get On', a national promotion campaign, was launched in autumn 2001 in order to attract learners to adult LLN programmes.

The new national standards are set at three levels, Entry Level, Level 1 and Level 2. The Entry Level is further sub-divided into three levels (Entry Level 1, 2 and 3). The standards for literacy cover the speaking, listening, reading and writing skills. The standards for numeracy cover the skills of interpreting, calculating and communicating mathematical information. The main purpose of the national standards is to provide a clear progression framework for learners and teachers, and to 'provide nationally agreed benchmarks against which the literacy, language and numeracy skills of the adult population can be assessed through national tests and national qualifications' (DfES 2002a). Since the introduction of the new qualifications and the matching curricula, all literacy, numeracy and ESOL teaching in the country is to be based on the standards. At present, national tests exist for Level 1 and 2, and at Entry Level a range of different qualifications is available.

Funding

The new national system has important consequences for the way adult language, literacy and numeracy education is funded. Since the introduction of Skills for Life, government funding for literacy, numeracy and ESOL provision is tied to the national frameworks. From September 2002 only those adult literacy qualifications that are based on the national standards and which have been accredited into the National Qualifications Framework by the QCA (Quality and Curriculum Authority) are eligible for funding by the Learning and Skills Council (the quango responsible for funding post-16 education throughout England). For providers (such as community-based colleges and projects) who would like to use other external – or their own internal – tests and qualifications it is now more difficult to receive funding from the government. However, the Learning and Skills Councils offer some funding for learners who are not ready to take the national tests and who will be non-externally assessed, provided their learning achievement is mapped to the national standards.

With regard to ESOL, the situation is slightly more complex. I have said there is a national curriculum for ESOL, but the government has made it clear that literacy and ESOL are part of the same system of national standards and qualifications, and there is some debate how far the ESOL curriculum was modelled on the Literacy curriculum (Ade-ojo 2004). A number of different qualifications exist. Some of those already in use prior to Skills for Life have been broadly aligned to the levels of the National Standards for Adult Literacy. In 2002, these were accredited by the QCA (for the academic years 2002–2004). The National Open College Network has produced new ESOL qualifications at entry levels 1–3 and Level 1, which are fully mapped to the national standards and to the new national ESOL curriculum. These are fully accredited.

The Pathfinders

As part of the introduction of the Skills for Life strategy, the government was keen to try out innovations in the delivery and form of provision. To this effect, in April 2001, nine so-called Pathfinder areas, one in each English region (plus one in the Prison Service), were established to test the new standards, curricula, teacher training and tests. The Pathfinders piloted various measures aimed at people who claim benefits. In Leeds and Wearside, for example, the use of financial incentives for learners' attendance at courses and tests taken were tested. In other Pathfinders, jobseekers were 'screened' (a form of quick assessment that is carried out by employees of job centres) when they first signed on, or at 13 weeks' unemployment. If their literacy and numeracy skills were found to be insufficient, they were required to participate in adult LLN classes. For those who did not join or dropped out without good reason, loss of their Job Seekers Allowance could result.

Following these pilot projects, the DfES put in place a range of assessment tools that can be used by colleges, employers and job centres to screen and diagnose people for their literacy and numeracy difficulties. Providers of adult LLN can now use initial assessment materials to help place new students in the appropriate level of course, and further materials for so-called 'diagnostic assessment' subsequently. These assessment instruments are based on the national qualifications. Following the first nine Pathfinders, eleven new Pathfinders for ESOL were set up in 2002, to test and develop the learning infrastructure for ESOL.

You can find more information about the implementation of the Skills for Life strategy, the standards and tests, and the Pathfinders on the Adult Basic Skills Strategy Unit's website: http://www.dfes.gov.uk/readwriteplus.

The effects of the new system

Without doubt, Skills for Life has not only raised the profile of adult LLN, but has greatly increased the potential for expansion of the sector. As a public service mandated by legislation, adult basic education had a secure institutional base – even before the launch of the new programme. But provision was not always sufficient to meet the demands from learners. Due to the government's increased commitment, a 'national learning infrastructure' (DfES 2002a), a coherent national strategy to improve adult literacy and numeracy skills, is now in place. With the new funding, provision has increased. After its first year of implementation, the government reported the first results of the programme: between April and October 2001 alone, 91,000 adults in England had improved their basic skills (DfES 2002a). By July 2002, the number of adults who had improved their literacy and numeracy skills had reached 300,000 (DfES 2003). A year on, this figure had risen to 470,000. For the first time, a National Research and Development Centre for Adult Literacy, Numeracy (NRDC) was created. The centre, co-ordinated by the Institute of Education in London, includes the universities of Lancaster, Nottingham and Sheffield, and other organisations.

Not surprisingly, many researchers and practitioners see Skills for Life as a unique moment of opportunity for adult literacy, numeracy and ESOL. The steady growth in enrolments is impressive and there is no doubt that an increasing number of people do improve their language, literacy and numeracy skills, as demonstrated by the learners who take and pass the national tests. There is little doubt also that the current government takes seriously its responsibility for the education of all citizens, children and adults included. This marks an important shift compared to the policies of the 1970s and 1980s when the state's commitment to adult language, literacy and numeracy was low.

The move from a patchy structure of opportunities and courses to a coherent 'infrastructure' (the term used by the government), with systematic and uniform standards, should be seen as a positive development, as it allows for greater transparency and accountability. A clear system of standards and progression routes makes it much easier for learners to have their achievements measured and recognised. According to some practitioners, with the earlier Wordpower and Numberpower framework, learners did not feel that they were progressing (Hamilton and Merrifield 2000). Some stayed for several years in the same class.

On the other hand, a national framework that insists on coherence and uniformity is likely to reduce the opportunity to develop programmes that directly respond to the specific demands of individuals and communities. Ever since the 1992 Further and Higher Education Act moved adult basic education into the formal sector of post-16 education, community-based programmes and 'alternative' visions (Hamilton 1998) have been pushed to the margin. The new policy has done little to reverse this trend.

With its Skills for Life policy, the government has clearly set out its priorities in terms of those who should receive support with their literacy, language and numeracy skills. Among these are public-sector employees with low skills, unem- ployed people and benefit claimants. The experience of practitioners suggests that some of these groups are relatively easy to reach and it is reasonable to assume that these make up a large percentage of the many new learners that join Skills for Life classes all over the country. Much is being done also to improve workplace- based provision and the developments in this area are certainly to be welcomed.

The Skills for Life programme has set out a strategy for the training and contin- uing professional development of adult language, literacy and numeracy teachers, the ultimate aim being for those working in the sector to reach the same level of qualifications as teachers in schools. Working towards giving adult LLN teachers greater opportunities for professional development can hardly be dismissed as a negative move. But teachers will critically judge these measures in terms of their quality, practical usefulness and links with career progression.

How practitioners and researchers have reacted to the new policy

It is still too early to know much about the success or the problems of the new strategy. An analysis of the policy itself, as in the previous section, provides insights into potential limitations and challenges. However, we need to go beyond the policy statements themselves and address the complex issue of what really gets implemented. How – in actual teaching practice – do learners and teachers react to and take up the policy? What is happening in adult LLN classes in England at the time of writing? What difference does the new curriculum make? How have teachers and learners incorporated it into their own understanding of reading and writing, and their own goals for literacy? Teachers and learners, and all those who implement the new policy, are not passive recipients of the dominant models of literacy that the Skills for Life programme aims to prescribe. They are actively involved in turning the policy into reality, and in the process they certainly affect what is happening.

Even before Skills for Life was launched, a vivid debate about the state of adult literacy, numeracy and ESOL in England – and the UK generally – had begun. On the whole, comments by practitioners, researchers and local organisations involved in adult language, literacy and numeracy education indicate that the shift in the agenda of literacy – that began in the late 1980s and led to Skills for Life – receives highly mixed reactions from those involved in the field of adult basic education. For many, the conception of adult basic education in terms of pre-vocational and vocational literacy and numeracy skills fails to recognise people's existing uses of literacy, the skills they possess or the meanings that literacy has for them. Therefore, invariably it results in a deficit view, which focuses on what people can't do, rather than on what they do already (Crowther, Hamilton and Tett 2001).

While the current framework empowers the dominant concepts of literacy, it disempowers people's own views and their own specific demands for improved reading and writing. Individual and everyday literacy and numeracy practices go far beyond what is vocationally relevant. But the Skills for Life policy is strikingly silent about people's own reading and writing practices.

Many practitioners feel under much pressure to deliver the content and activities covered in the curriculum and to prepare students to take the national tests. But are these necessarily the kind of literacies that are relevant to learners' everyday lives? On a more general level, this begs the question: how many learners want to achieve a qualification? And what influence do the tests and standards have on what is taught and how we teach? Do we end up teaching to the test (see Lavender, Derrick and Brooks 2004)? And, finally, what really do the tests measure? What do they tell us about what people have learned and what difference this has made to their lives?

A social view of literacy invites us to raise a number of questions about the usefulness and the appropriateness of tests. Can they take account of current under-standings of literacy as plural and diverse rather than singular and universal? How can tests cover different literacies? Another question is how tests can assess what people do with literacy. From a social literacies perspective, this is more crucial than knowing how many words (in theory) a person can write. The underlying question is whether the skills of reading, writing and calculating can be detached from the purposes within which this reading, writing and calculating is being done. And, finally, what about the wider benefits of learning on people's lives? How can these be captured?

Others have noted that the new framework, while suitable for many, is not appropriate for those learners who are put off by screening and diagnosis, tests and standards. They argue that there has always been a group of people who were difficult to reach through standard college-based provision and that the new system has done nothing to make education more appealing to this group. The danger is that Skills for Life, with its focus on mainstream values and procedures, its common curriculum and its many schooled literacy practices (for example, tests), will exclude those who are not part of the mainstream and who would never get close to a college. What for example does Skills for Life do to reach the long-term unemployed?

Developments in other parts of the UK

In their comments on the new policy, practitioners and researchers have also looked to the development of adult LLN policy in other countries. Tendencies towards a strong vocational agenda for literacy and numeracy are widespread in industrialised countries. Interestingly, the situation is not the same everywhere in the countries of the UK. Scotland and Northern Ireland have seen similar moves towards a strong economic and vocational focus, but in both cases the sector has developed in a slightly different way from that in England. Whereas in Northern Ireland and England adult basic education is part of the formal structure of post-16 education, in Scotland the main provider of adult basic education is the community education sector, run by local education authorities.

Funding in Scotland for adult literacy, numeracy and ESOL comes out of the Lifelong Learning budget and this provides the ground for developing LLN beyond 'basic skills'. The government institution that has overall responsibility for literacy, numeracy and ESOL is Communities Scotland, a branch of the Scottish Executive dealing with housing and regeneration. On the whole, in Scotland, adult LLN is more strongly placed within the policy goals of lifelong learning, social inclusion and active citizenship. This agenda is potentially broader than the concerns that dominate literacy policy in England and may open the way for more diversified and learner-centred provisions. In a similar way, government documents in Northern Ireland conceive of literacy in a broader sense, encompassing more than vocational skills. There, most programmes are informal and run by volunteers. There is little central control of programmes.

There is also a striking difference in the terminology used in England and Scotland. Communities Scotland talks about 'adult literacies' in plural, while the DfES uses the singular form. On its website (www.communitiesscotland.gov.uk), the agency defines adult literacies as

> The ability to read and write and use numeracy, to handle information, to express ideas and opinions, to make decisions and solve problems, as family members, workers, citizens and lifelong learners. (accessed 26 August 2004)

Further below on the same page, literacy and numeracy are recognised as 'complex capabilities rather than a simple set of basic skills'.

Despite these apparent differences between the Scottish and the English systems, there are also similarities. Scotland is now developing a national curriculum, one of its aims being to facilitate the ways students' progress can be assessed. As part of this, it is intended that core skills can be incorporated into the Scottish Credit and Qualifications Framework (SCQF). These developments appear to move the policy towards a system that is similar to Skills for Life.

Reading

DfES (2003b) *Skills for Life: The National Strategy for Improving Adult Literacy and Numeracy Skills, Focus on Delivery 2007*, pp. 2–10

Skills for Life

The national strategy for improving adult literacy and numeracy skills

Focus on delivery to 2007

Foreword

by the Rt Hon Charles Clarke MP, Secretary of State for Education and Skills

When the Prime Minister first launched *Skills for Life* in March 2001, we set ourselves formidable targets for helping adults improve their literacy, language and numeracy skills.

We want 750,000 adults to improve their literacy, language and numeracy skills by 2004, and I am happy to say that we have already made good progress to achieve that goal: more than quarter of a million people have achieved national certificates.

What's more, I was able to announce in November 2002 that we are to invest record spending of £1.6 billion across Government over the next three years. This should enable 1.5 million adults to significantly improve their reading, writing and maths skills by 2007.

So far, so good. It might be tempting to become complacent.

But there are still millions of adults in this country who lack the reading and maths skills that we expect of the average 11-year-old. According to Sir Claus Moser's landmark report, *A Fresh Start*, one in five adults, if given the alphabetical index to the Yellow Pages, cannot locate the page reference for plumbers. And one in three adults in this country cannot calculate the area of a room that is 21 by 14 feet, even with the aid of a calculator.

Consider the wider impact that lacking such skills has on an adult's life. Having poor essential skills means having a lower income (on average £50,000 less over your working life) and being less employable. It is not surprising that this condition compounds the problems of poor health, crime and living in disadvantaged areas.

This revised version of *Skills for Life* sets out what we have already achieved and more importantly, what we still have to do by 2007 to make an impact on these problems.

It also sets out how *Skills for Life* is contributing to the new *Skills Strategy* that will be announced in July 2003.

We must build on the excellent work we have started to raise the standard of teaching provision and learning achievements. We can be proud of the foundations we have laid for a robust national learning and teaching framework.

We have produced new guidance to improve standards across the board in further education. In 2002 we launched *Success for All*, our strategy for transforming further education, which aims to build a more effective and responsive learning and skills sector and raise standards, supported by the largest ever investment programme in further education and training.

In addition to continuing to raise standards we have to enhance the status of vocational education and training as a high quality route to progression and achievement for young people.

In Britain today we face an increasingly demanding and fast-moving world of business.

So it is absolutely essential that education prepares learners for work. Four out of five jobs created now will require skill levels above A-level. Only one-third of Britons have these compared to three-quarters of Germans. It's not just the learner's personal success that hangs in the balance. What of the cost to British business? Poor literacy, language and numeracy skills are estimated to cost the country well in excess of £10 billion a year. That is why we are ensuring that all staff that need it in any business can get free training to improve their skills, with a new employer campaign to raise the profile of skills in the workplace.

We have begun to roll out National Tests in literacy and numeracy – new benchmarks in learner achievement. They are essential for learners' personal satisfaction and for improving their employability.

And with the rapid rate at which information technology is changing business, adults need more than ever to equip themselves with computer skills. In partnership with awarding bodies there are now versions of the on-screen national tests.

As ever, promotion will be crucial to our success. No qualification will get learners very far unless it is recognised by employers.

This document sets out our commitment to continue this good work. But we will not have an impact unless we can engage potential learners and provide learning opportunities in ways and places that meet their needs – be it at home, work or elsewhere.

We must continue to approach partnerships imaginatively. Only then can we reach learners and give them the support they need to enjoy happier futures.

Summary

The challenge

1   Dozens of times every day, each of us needs to read, write and use numbers. Whether we are reading a newspaper or the instructions on a medicine bottle, using a bus or train timetable, or working out whether we can afford to buy something, not being able to understand written words or numbers could make our day a source of worry and stress. Millions of people have to cope with these very difficulties. The ground-breaking report, *A Fresh Start*, published in March 1999, following the review chaired by Sir Claus Moser, identified up to 7 million adults in England who cannot read or write at the level we would expect of an 11-year-old. Even more have trouble with numbers.

2   Of course, people with these poor literacy, language and numeracy skills get by, usually by relying on others for help or by avoiding situations where they need to read, write or calculate. But, because they lack literacy, language and numeracy skills, they and their families may well be excluded from advantages that others take for granted. Or they may be in low-paid or short-term jobs or suffer lengthy periods of unemployment. Even after taking into account all other factors that influence earnings, people with inadequate literacy skills earn on average 11% less than their better skilled colleagues, whilst people with inadequate numeracy skills earn on average 6% to 7% less.[1] This means that you could be £50,000 worse off over your working life if you have poor literacy, language and numeracy skills.[2]

3   As well as losing out financially, people with literacy, language and numeracy skills deficiencies may have low self-confidence and low motivation. Their children are more likely to struggle at school. And they are more prone to health problems and to suffer social exclusion. New technology is significantly increasing the need to read, write and use numbers confidently and effectively. Before long, those who cannot use a computer and access the internet may be as disadvantaged as those who are now unable to write or add up, and information technology skills are as fundamental as literacy, language or numeracy skills.

4   The effect of poor literacy, language and numeracy skills on individuals is severe. But there is a cost to society that is just as great. Employers, in particular, cannot compete in an increasingly global, knowledge-based economy without a workforce able to add real value at every level. One in five employers reports a significant gap in their workers' skills. And over a third of those companies with a literacy, language or numeracy skills gap say that they have lost business or orders to competitors because of it. Combining the effect of lower incomes, reduced productivity, poorer health and the cost of consequential benefits and

welfare services, some have estimated the cost to the country of poor literacy, language and numeracy skills to be as high as £10 billion a year.[3]

Meeting the challenge – delivering *Skills for Life*

5 Tackling this skills problem is one of the Government's key priorities. Our goal is to reduce the number of adults in England with literacy, language and numeracy difficulties to the levels of our main international competitors – that is from one in five adults to one in ten or better. We aim to help 750,000 adults achieve national certificates by 2004, and to help 1.5 million achieve the same by 2007.

6 We should not stop there. The aim of any civilised society, as *A Fresh Start* recognised, must be the virtual elimination of poor literacy, language and numeracy. Only bold and imaginative policies, engaging those who can make a real difference in the workplace and communities, can change this cultural inheritance.

We need, for example, to work with employers to ensure that enhanced skills help improve business performance. The Government's white paper "21st Century Skills: Realising our Potential" published in July 2003 confirmed *Skills for Life* as providing the foundation for skills development. It announced that ICT would be included within *Skills For Life* as the third basic skill and confirmed that literacy and numeracy skills are to be embedded in the definition of full level 2 qualifications.

The Skills Strategy puts forward an agenda for working in partnership with employers. The aim is to ensure that the skills we develop are valuable to young people and adults and valued by employers.

The key themes within the strategy are:

- Putting employers needs centre stage and creating a more 'demand-led' system;
- Helping employers use skills to achieve more ambitious, longer-term business success;
- Motivating and supporting learners – making it easier for those adults who most need extra skills by offering a new entitlement to learning;
- Enabling colleges and training providers to be more responsive to employers' and learners' needs by reviewing the framework for planning, funding and monitoring provision; and
- Joint Government action in a new Skills Alliance, linking up the work of key Government departments involved with economic and Skills issues.

7 *Skills for Life* builds upon the success of the daily literacy and mathematics lessons that have transformed the quality of teaching in primary schools and the new

strategies for Key Stage 3. It also links with broader government policies, such as the commitment to Neighbourhood Renewal, to tackle the problems faced by deprived communities, and the findings of the Adult Financial Literacy Advisory Group, which identified how people can improve their skills when managing their personal finances. Our goal to improve young people's literacy and numeracy skills is also central to the new *Opportunity and Excellence* 14–19 strategy.

8 We must be clear about how to tackle the skills problem. All those involved in literacy, language and numeracy skills teaching are working towards a common goal in four key areas:

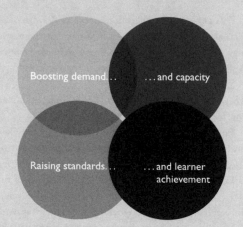

Boosting demand

9 Boosting demand for learning through effective promotion and engaging Government agencies and employers to identify and address the literacy, language and numeracy needs of their clients and employees.

Ensuring capacity

10 Increasing the capacity of provision by securing sufficient funding and co-ordinating planning and delivery to meet learners' needs.

Raising standards

11 Improving the quality of teaching in literacy, numeracy and English for Speakers of Other Languages (ESOL) provision through the national teaching, learning and assessment infrastructure.

Learner achievement

12 Increasing learner achievement through the national teaching, learning and assessment infrastructure, the numbers of young people and adults succeeding in national qualifications and reducing barriers to learning. It is not enough just to help them reach levels of functional literacy, language and numeracy. Our strategy aims to improve their skills up to and including Level 2 of the National Qualifications Framework, whether they choose to follow programmes leading to qualifications in literacy or numeracy or key skills.

13 These measures represent a huge challenge to all those working with people who could improve their literacy, language and numeracy skills. Our strategy requires nothing less than a cultural transformation among adults and a radical improvement in the quality of the training and support delivered to them. So our strategy depends upon the successful implementation of *Success for All*, which is set to reform all post-16 learning. None of this can be achieved by one agency alone, nor just by Government. We can only succeed in tackling this problem through shared goals.

Our priority groups

14 Identifying the one in five adults with poor literacy, language and numeracy skills, and bringing them back into learning, is vital. We know from existing research that literacy, language and numeracy difficulties are more common among certain groups. To impact on skills needs, we must continue to get help to these groups first.

15 At least a third of unemployed people, for example, have literacy skills at no more than Level 1 – the level we expect of an 11-year-old. And over a third of people with poor literacy, language and numeracy skills are in receipt of social security benefits (excluding pensions and child benefit), compared with less than one in ten of those with better developed skills.[4] Research also shows that those working in low-skilled occupations have much poorer literacy, language and numeracy ability. These shortcomings are also closely associated with other factors including homelessness or living in disadvantaged communities.

16 Our strategy addresses these groups as a matter of urgency, particularly:

- Unemployed people and benefit claimants
- Prisoners and those supervised in the community
- Employees – public sector, low-skilled, young adults
- Other groups at risk of exclusion, including speakers of other languages and those in disadvantaged communities.

17 For those groups in regular receipt of state support, such as jobseekers and benefit claimants, as well as for those detained in penal institutions, the Government is acting quickly to identify literacy, language and numeracy skills needs and to remedy them. Through its various agencies, the Government has direct contact with people in these groups and is using that opportunity to encourage them to develop their literacy, language and numeracy skills.

18 We are also addressing the skills gap in the workforce more widely. Of the 7 million adults in England with literacy, language and numeracy needs, we estimate that up to half have jobs. Many are in low-skilled or short-term employment. We must increase their earnings potential by giving them the skills they need to participate in a global, knowledge-based economy. Our strategy engages with employers, trade unions and others to ensure that all those in low-skilled work are given the opportunities they need to improve their skills.

19 Furthermore, an Adult Basic Skills Needs Survey, that will provide insights by region and by priority group area, is due to be published in the autumn of 2003. It will help us to identify where our resources should be going.

Figure 1: Literacy, language and numeracy skills strategy

Our strategy targets those in key priority groups with literacy, language and numeracy needs:

Those with literacy, language and numeracy needs in regular contact with government and its agencies, comprising around:	Around 200,000 public sector employees with literacy, language and numeracy needs in:	Approximately 1.5 million low-skilled people in employment with literacy, language and numeracy needs, particularly:	Other groups at high risk of exclusion due to poor literacy, language and numeracy skills, including:
• 250,000 unemployed people • 1.5 million other benefit claimants • 300,000 prisoners and those supervised in the community	• Central government • Local government • Armed Forces • National Health Service	• Those in occupations and sectors with low average literacy, language and numeracy rates • Young people in employment	• Around 60,000 homeless people with literacy, language and numeracy needs • Up to 1 million refugees, asylum seekers and others who do not speak English as their first language • Parents with poor skills, including around 250,000 lone parents with no qualifications • Around 1.7 million adults with literacy, language and numeracy needs who live in disadvantaged communities

Learners' needs are identified, addressed and monitored by government agencies and partners, including:

• Jobcentre Plus • Benefits Agency • Health services • Community and voluntary organisations • Prison Service	• Public sector employers	• Employers • Trade unions • National training organisations • Small Business Service • Connexions Service	• Local Authorities • Residents' Associations • Learning partnerships • Local Learning and Skills Councils

- Probation Service

- Jobcentre Plus programmes
- Social Services
- Sector Skills Councils

- Voluntary and community organisations
- Religious bodies
- Health services
- Refugee Council and similar bodies
- Age Concern and similar charities
- Football clubs
- Libraries
- Information, Advice and Guidance Partnerships

Free training is being provided through:

- Dedicated provision e.g. family literacy programmes for parents
- Full-time courses, including intensive 'booster' courses
- Part-time courses
- Self-study, 'mentored' learning and *learndirect*

By 2004, our strategy will improve the literacy, language and numeracy skills of 750,000 adults in England, comprising approximately:

- 130,000 jobseekers
- 40,000 other benefit claimants
- 40,000 prisoners and others supervised in the community

- 10,000 public sector employees

- 50,000 adults in low-skilled jobs
- 110,000 young people

- 210,000 general literacy and numeracy skills learners including those on *learndirect* courses
- 50,000 refugees and speakers of other languages
- 60,000 parents
- 50,000 people who live in disadvantaged communities

By 2007, our strategy will improve the literacy, language and numeracy skills of 1.5 million adults in England, comprising approximately:

- 220,000 jobseekers
- 100,000 other benefit claimants
- 80,000 prisoners and others supervised in the community

- 20,000 public sector employees

- 150,000 adults in low-skilled jobs
- 170,000 young people

- 420,000 general literacy and numeracy skills learners including those on *learndirect* courses
- 100,000 refugees and speakers of other languages
- 120,000 parents
- 150,000 people who live in disadvantaged communities

Charlotte Brady

Just over a year ago Charlotte, 18, from Leamington Spa, was unemployed, unable to read or write and lacked self-confidence.

That has now all changed for the better, thanks to Charlotte enrolling on a Basic Skills course with Rathbone training providers.

On the course Charlotte discovered the joy of reading, quickly finding part-time employment as a housekeeper in a nearby Care Home, whilst still meeting with Basic Skills training adviser Lindy Thomas every Thursday afternoon.

To celebrate her achievement Charlotte was chosen as a national Rathbone learner of the month in 2002, winning a dream tour to Old Trafford to walk on the pitch and visit the Manchester United changing rooms, including the locker of her hero David Beckham.

Said Lindy: "Charlotte came to Rathbone with the opinion that she was stupid, but she has now found her own place to live, learnt valuable budgeting skills, and has a real thirst for reading out-loud, as well as enjoying learning how to use a computer."

"She has been working extremely hard with her reading and is now able to create her own CV and it is great to see she is now nearing the completion of the first few stages of her NVQ Level 1."

Charlotte will now attend the 2002 Rathbone Learner of the Year awards, hoping to scoop the national title.

Reflection

When you have read through the extracts from the *Skills for Life* document, you can try the following questions and tasks:

1   What discourses about literacy can you find in the text?
2   How are the people whom the new policy addresses described? How are they represented (e.g. by using generic terms)? What does the text say about their situation and their needs? Are any reasons given for why they have difficulties with reading and writing?
3   Have a look at the summary of the *Skills for Life* document on pages 106–10. Look at some of the grammatical aspects of the text: What does the use of words like 'must', 'would' and 'could' tell you about the meaning of particular sentences and paragraphs? How are active and passive voice employed and what is the effect of this on how social actors are represented? How are the pronouns 'we' and 'our' used (inclusively or exclusively)?
4   Judging from the text (as well as from your own experience), would you say that the policy privileges certain literacy and numeracy practices? Which ones are these?

5   What do you think are the biggest challenges for practitioners since the introduction of the Skills for Life policy?

Additional reading

Black, S. (2004) 'Whose economic wellbeing? A challenge to dominant discourses on the relationship between literacy/numeracy skills and (un)employment', *Literacy and Numeracy Studies* 13 (1): 7–17.

Crowther, J., Hamilton, M. and Tett, L. (2001) 'Powerful literacies: an introduction', in J. Crowther, M. Hamilton and L. Tett (eds) *Powerful Literacies*, Leicester: NIACE, pp. 1–13.

Chapter 7

A critical reading of the Skills for Life strategy

What this chapter is about

In this chapter, I take a closer look at the Skills for Life strategy itself, as it has been spelled out – in the initial policy papers and in subsequently produced reports and strategic plans. The purpose of this chapter is to provide a critical reading of the main discourses that have informed the policy and this complements the more general discussion of Skills for Life in Chapter 6.

What I will do is to provide snapshots of a critical reading of some of these papers and reports. By 'critical' I mean a reading that unveils the views about literacy, numeracy and ESOL that underpin the strategy and what these say about the learners and their assumed learning needs and aspirations. What discourse of literacy, for example, underpins the new emphasis on tests? Furthermore, I want to ask whether the policy discourses that dominate Skills for Life match the discourses of literacy used by learners and teachers, and what this can tell us about how teachers and learners react to and work with the new system (or don't work with it, in the case of those who 'refuse' to be attracted by the government's powerful 'Get on' campaign).

The aim of this exercise in critical reading is not to dismiss the current policy, but to make us aware of its presuppositions and claims – and then, based on these insights, to begin to think about its challenges and limitations as well as about alternatives to the dominant approach.

The approach I take is mostly a content analysis of policy documents, but I also draw on work done in the interdisciplinary field of Critical Discourse Analysis (CDA). The linguist Norman Fairclough (2003), among others, has developed an elaborate framework to examine the relations between a text's linguistic features (including grammatical aspects such as modes, and lexis) and its semantic properties. To put it more simply, his method allows us to examine how particular discourses (in the way I defined them earlier in this book) are manifested linguistically and how the linguistic properties of a text favour specific ('dominant') readings of it.

The method of CDA, when applied in full, is highly productive and there is no scope for such comprehensive work here. Traditionally, discourse analysts choose a small number of texts, or just a single document, which they then analyse in detail. For the present purpose, I draw on a series of documents produced by the DfES since 2001 and I examine one brief text in greater detail. The documents I have chosen are listed in the references at the end of this chapter and they are available on the DfES readwriteplus website.

The role of statistical evidence in the Skills for Life strategy

We have already seen that there has been a growth in enrolments and qualifications passed since the introduction of Skills for Life. A closer look at the first *Skills for Life* document (DfEE 2001b) reveals the central role that literacy statistics have played in the development and implementation of the new strategy. This document was the first in a series of strategic papers, bi-annual reports and newsletters produced by ABSSU after the launch of the new strategy in 2001. The document, an A4-sized brochure of 67 pages, explains the government's reasons for investing in Skills for Life and sets out the main aspects of the new strategy. It also contains a series of narratives and portraits of individual learners, the latter illustrated by photographs.

Statistical knowledge of the number of people supposedly having problems with reading, writing and mathematics serves as a justification for the need to commit increased effort to adult basic education. In his foreword to the document, David Blunkett writes about the 'shocking' 7 million adults who 'cannot read and write at the level we would expect of an 11-year-old' (DfEE 2001b: 7). Numerical targets figure strongly in the expected outcomes of the strategy, as detailed in the text. The formulation of policy goals in numerical terms is common in government policies and we all know about league tables and performance targets. In England, such pledges are the government's response to a highly publicised debate about falling literacy standards and the country's standing in the world.

The Skills for Life document and other related publications frequently quote from the International Adult Literacy Survey (IALS), which was conducted by the Organisation for Economic Co-operation and Development (OECD). Since the publication of its results in 1995 and 2000 (OECD 1995, 2000), the IALS (with other surveys; see, for example, Bynner and Parsons 1997) has had a strong influence on the development of adult basic education policy in the UK and elsewhere in the industrialised world. The main aim of the IALS was to produce meaningful statistics of literacy levels in each country, and so allow comparison between countries. The British government has used these comparisons, which put England behind countries such as Sweden or Canada, in order to alert voters to the issue of adult literacy and to justify the government's commitment to the sector.

In government reports and policy papers, statistical evidence is frequently employed to back up political decisions. Such texts also use generalised comparisons between different states of affairs or different groups of people. An example is the above quotation from the then Minister of Education. His words establish a direct comparison between the reading and writing of children and adults. By using children's literacy as the default value, the statement immediately distorts adult competencies and experiences. It assumes that there is one autonomous skill – literacy – that can meaningfully be applied to all sorts of people and situations. The intent here is to shock and to make the public aware of a 'problem' that the government is keen to tackle.

Fairclough (2003: 94–95) describes a common feature of many contemporary policy texts: they follow a 'logic of appearances', not a logic of explanation. They provide descriptive accounts of states of affairs or changes, without explaining how these came about. In our case, the state of affairs reported is that 7 million adults cannot read and write at the level of an 11-year-old. This is presented simply as given, with no explanation as to how the '7 million adults' or the 'level of an 11-year-old' were identified. Whether it is appropriate to compare adults' reading and writing with children's literacy is not questioned. Furthermore, no attempt is made to explain what might have caused this situation. This seemingly innocuous statement is built on a whole set of assumptions, none of which is made explicit in the text.

The above touches upon the much broader debate over the appropriateness and validity of literacy tests. What do surveys such as IALS really measure (Hamilton and Barton 2000)? And what is the power of their results, once these are reported in government papers and speeches? A further question to ask is what concept of literacy underpins such tests. IALS without doubt is built on a concept of literacy and numeracy as discrete skills. Such skills can be measured by administering tasks that test performance on isolated competencies. This is strikingly different from a social practices view of literacy; I will come back to this question later in this chapter.

'Improving adult basic skills, addressing a generation of neglect'

In 2003, the government commissioned its own 'mini' IALS, a survey (of 8,730 adults, aged 16–65) to 'assess' the literacy and numeracy skills of the population. Like IALS, this survey aimed to reveal the links between low levels of skills, unemployment and low wages. A brief report that summarises the findings of the survey is available on the ABSSU website (*Improving Adult Basic Skills, Addressing a Generation of Neglect*, posted 3 November 2003). A copy of the report can be found at the end of this chapter. I now briefly examine this document.

The two-page text can be divided roughly into four parts. The first section explains what the survey is about. The second part presents, in bullet points, the 'key findings' of the survey. The third section consists of two ministerial quotes that serve to illustrate the government's commitment to adult basic education. The final section, again presented in the form of bullet points, lists what other measures (in addition to Skills for Life) the government has initiated in order to support adult skills. There are also some notes for newspaper editors.

The first section: the survey as the dominant voice

The headline and first section set the tone for the remainder of this brief document. Particularly noticeable is that the top paragraph presents the survey as the first 'definitive national profile of adult literacy and numeracy skills', the use of the word 'definitive' aiming to convey a picture of the survey as a true and objective representation of the nation's skills. The first paragraph is visually emphasised by using bold characters and a larger font. This serves to attract readers' attention to what could be seen as a summary of what the government considers to be the main result of the survey: it demonstrates the existence of a literacy 'problem' and thus justifies and supports the government's policy. Note also that the survey is of course covering just a sample of people, so it can be seen as 'representative of the nation', but cannot be 'national' in the stricter sense of the word.

Nothing is said in this first section, or indeed in the whole document, about the survey itself. The notes to editors at the end of the text contain some very brief information about the conduct of the survey, excluding, however, any information on the kind of test that was used to measure literacy and numeracy levels. This is another example of a logic of appearances, in a sense letting the figures talk for themselves.

Throughout the first section, the dominant voice is 'the survey'. This draws the reader's attention to the survey's findings, not to the survey itself (as a process or an instrument which was used by researchers to produce the results reported here). By focusing on the survey as a result or a state of affairs, it is treated as having agency, as having a voice. This is demonstrated in the following quotations:

> The survey demonstrates early success in the Government's drive to increase the numbers of adults with basic skills in literacy and numeracy.

> The survey underlines the need for the Government to continue its successful 'Skills for Life' programme, which has already seen over 1.8 million adults start basic skills courses.

In both quotations, we could replace the first three words by 'The results of the survey show', though this still attributes agency to the survey itself; whereas, if we replaced the first three words of either sentence by 'the researchers who carried out the survey found', we would clearly assign agency to those who conducted the survey, thereby treating the survey itself as what it really is: an instrument or a tool used by people for certain ends.

The effect of presenting the survey as the agent is similar to what Fairclough describes happening in the case of 'nominalisations' (Fairclough 2003: 44–45, 225). These are metaphorical representations of a process as a noun. This is achieved when a phrase that describes activity is turned into a noun that has agency and therefore can be attributed with responsibility and authority. An example Fairclough uses is 'globalisation'. I will come back to nominalisation later in this chapter.

The second section: how different actors are represented

In the second section of this short report, I want to look at how different actors are represented and who is given voice and agency. In the second section, the dominant voice is that of 'men' and 'women' in general, as here:

> Men and women have similar levels of literacy, but men appear to have higher levels of numeracy.

The total number of respondents is given at the beginning of this section, but not mentioned again. A different way of writing the sentence above could have been: 'The men and women who took part in the survey had similar literacy levels'. Instead the generic form is used. This is abstract and suggests that what counts for those included in the survey can equally be attributed to the rest of the population. In this way, the DfES implicitly claims that the survey is representative.

   In later statements of the same section, the social actors are completely removed from the presentation of the survey results, as in the following sentence:

> Lower levels of literacy and numeracy were associated with socio-economic deprivation.

In the above sentence, the process of generalisation is taken even further. The people who were found to have low levels of skills are still the subject-matter of the sentence, but they are no longer its subject. The statement is turned into an abstract fact, not a matter of people and their attributes. The use of the passive voice further reinforces this, associating the sentence with scientific reports, a genre that makes frequent use of the passive in a similar attempt to claim objectivity. The use of the passive voice also obscures the agency of the people who established the correlations that are reported.

   The third section of the document is marked by an interesting change in tone and voice from the distanced 'objectivity' of the previous section to a more personalised style. Now, an individual person is named and his voice can be heard. The Minister of Skills and Vocational Education, Ivan Lewis, is quoted as saying:

> **I** am determined to ensure that today's young people will no longer endure the decades of neglect in literacy and numeracy education which is reflected so starkly in this survey. [my emphasis]

This is a strongly personalised statement. In contrast to the way social actors were presented in the previous section, the main actor here is foregrounded. The minister is named and his position is specified. The pronoun 'I' is used to signal the minister's identification with and commitment to the policy he describes; in this case, individual agency is not obfuscated, but purposely emphasised. The government, through the personalised voice of the minister, declares its commit-ment to and responsibility for adult literacy and numeracy education.

The next quotation from the minister begins like this:

> And **our** Skills for Life programme is now giving adults the chance to get the basic skills they need to get on and succeed. [my emphasis]

This is another personalised statement: this time it is the entire government that is declaring its commitment to adult literacy and numeracy education. The use of the pronoun 'our' (instead of the article 'the') serves to create a direct link between the government and the Skills for Life programme, emphasising that it is the government, by its work, that makes Skills for Life possible.

In both quotations, the pronouns 'we' and 'our' refer to the government, which presents itself here not as an impersonalised institution, but as people who act in support of those identified as experiencing difficulties with literacy and numeracy. Using 'we' can also be seen as an attempt at a more informal and personal tone. 'We', the people in the government, are 'acting' (thus the government grammat-ically is the subject and the dominant verb form is active, not passive): 'we' are doing something to alleviate the problem that 'we' identified. The implicit message here is that 'we' – the government – are doing something for 'you' – the people who read this report.

In the last section, the text reverts to the more impersonal style of the earlier sections. Another list of bullet points is presented, this time giving brief information on other measures the government is putting in place to support the development of literacy and numeracy skills among adults. The desired effect of the list is to impress by the number and range of measures.

Much more could be said about this particular text, but I want to stop here and continue to discuss the issues already raised, by bringing in statements from other documents produced by the DfES in its efforts to inform the public on the Skills for Life strategy.

Literacy – an economic perspective

Both the IALS and the government's more recent survey aimed to demonstrate the link between poverty and low skills. The rationale for this was the need to provide policy-makers and planners with data that would explain the relationship between education, literacy and income. The link between literacy and vocational skills on the one hand, and employability and income on the other, is a strong theme in the Skills for Life strategy and it is referred to frequently in government reports and papers on the strategy. At the heart of the arguments made are the dis-advantages those with inappropriate literacy and numeracy skills are believed to experience in the job market. This is the dominant discourse about literacy, one which is strongly represented in public discussion. It sees lack of literacy as a major constraining factor in economic development, which weakens the country's ability to compete in the global economy and is a burden not only to individuals and communities, but to the entire nation.

Statements such as the following illustrate the economic perspective that frames the Skills for Life strategy:

> Poor basic skills cost the country as much as £10 billion per year in lost revenue, lower productivity and the increased burden on the state.
>
> (John Healey, Minister for Adult Skills,
> in: Update 2, DfES, winter 2002, p. 8)

This is another good example of Fairclough's logic of appearances. Once again, no explanations are given as to how poor basic skills cause low productivity and result in a burden on the state. To be fair, other documents produced by the government are much more precise on this and try to establish a direct relationship between low levels of skills and a weak economy, describing the negative consequences for individuals, companies and the nation at large. However, many of these seemingly more 'explanatory' accounts (Fairclough 2003) rely heavily on statistics (as in the above report on the survey) and present statistical correlation as causation. Others present generalised accounts of the difficulties people with low levels of skills are assumed to experience without any reference to the source of such insights.

Similar statements to John Healey's can be found in many of the subsequent documents published by Skills for Life. At times, these are turned around to emphasise the positive side of the assumed link, as in the following extract from the *Skills for Life Annual Review 2003–2004*, referring to the same survey discussed above:

> Critically, the survey found a significant earnings return to those with higher skills levels. For example, adults with Level 2 or above in numeracy were found to earn (on average) roughly twice the average annual income of those with skills at Entry level 1 or below.
>
> (*Skills for Life, Annual Review 2003–2004*, DfES, 2004, p. 4)

Comparisons with other industrialised countries appear several times in the Skills for Life documents (see, for example, DfEE 2001b: 8, 23), reflecting the government's concern for the country's position within the world economy. Reference is made to the 'global, knowledge based economy' and the assertion is made that people need improved literacy and numeracy skills in order to be able to participate in this global economy (DfEE 2001b: 11). The implicit inference is that the reason for people's inability to participate is their lack of skills. There is no mention of any other factors that cause people to be excluded from the knowledge economy and this is certainly an oversimplification of a complex issue, in which many inter-related factors play a role. Again, the logic of the extract is not explanatory, but expository.

Poor literacy and numeracy skills are blamed in part for the low productivity of the British economy (DfEE 2001b: 23). The losses that are assumed to result from poor literacy and numeracy skills are expressed mainly in terms of the economic cost to the country and individuals (see the quotation above). This borders on a discourse of responsibility that makes individuals accountable for the country's economic difficulties.

Yet again, as the following extract from the Foreword to the first Skills for Life document (DfEE 2001b) by David Blunkett illustrates, the official presentation follows a logic of appearances where changes in the social order are simply portrayed as given and irreversible:

> **We** live, at the beginning of the twenty-first century, in a society of challenge and opportunity. The **growth of the knowledge economy** and the **spread of information technology** are having a more profound and more rapid effect on our work and home lives than any other social change since the Industrial Revolution.' [my emphasis]

The second sentence of the above contains two further examples of how processes are being nominalised and thereby presented as things that have come about and whose significance and force is taken for granted. The growing knowledge economy and spreading information technology are represented as active forces responsible for social and economic change, obfuscating the work of human actors – who, by using technologies and altering their work practices, have made these changes happen. By turning a phrase that describes a process (e.g., people make more and more use of information technology) into a noun (that expresses a state), the technology is ascribed power, as if it was the technology that had led to social change, not the people using it. This also presents the process as inevitable and the results as having to be faced.

A little further down, Blunkett continues:

> The prosperity of the nation and every one of **us** depends on how we meet these challenges and opportunities.

Pronouns such as 'we' and 'us' can be used inclusively or exclusively (see Fairclough 2003, pp. 145 ff.) and the people they include or exclude may change within the same text. In the above extracts, both 'we' and 'us' are inclusive, aiming to draw in the potential reader (or the listener, in the original speech): the changes described concern everyone. No one can turn their eyes away from the knowledge economy. By comparison, in the brief report of the Skills for Life survey that I examined earlier, 'we' was used more exclusively to refer to the government in its efforts to promote basic skills.

How the policy speaks about learners

A final feature of the Skills for Life documents that I briefly want to discuss here is how they talk about learners and about those who are assumed to have literacy and numeracy difficulties. The first Skills for Life document of 2001 (a and b) (as well as other publications) makes frequent references to the apparent lack of motivation and the reluctance of those who have difficulties with literacy and numeracy to come forward to adult basic education classes (see, for example, DfES 2002: 11).

The *Skills for Life: Annual Review 2003–2004* devotes a whole section to the need for the government to 'stimulate demand' for learning. The same section reports on the government's achievements in promoting demand for learning through the Get On campaign. Clearly not all those addressed by the campaign have joined classes, but there is no mention of the reasons they may have for not joining. People's needs are assumed and the basis for such assumptions is provided by statistics such as the ones presented in the survey above. These assertions are accompanied by statements, which refer to people not being aware of their problems or not being willing to address them. These discourses portray people with assumed low levels of literacy, language and numeracy skills as passive and disengaged, and in some cases even dishonest.

In stark contrast to these silent bystanders are the many success stories of individual learners who joined Skills for Life and who – like Carole Reeve, whose achievements are presented in the 2003–4 annual review – have changed their lives. Ms Reeve is quoted as saying that she feels 'like a different person' (*Skills for Life: Annual Review 2003–2004*, DfES, 2004). Portraits of individual learners, accompanied by carefully staged and glossy photographs and a few catchy quotations, can be found frequently in the Skills for Life documents (see also the Reading for Chapter 6). They merit attention for the powerful way in which individual cases are used to provide evidence for the government's success and for the various discourses about literacy they contain. In Carole Reeve's case, this is a discourse of literacy as personal transformation. It is presented through a personalised account that gives voice to the individual learner (even if this is mostly a mediated voice, an account written in report style and using the third person). The quotes add authenticity to this narrative. By contrast, non-learners are not given any individual voice at all, but are referred to in generic categories (an example is 'low-skilled people in employment' on page 6 of the 2003–4 annual review).

Conclusion: a discourse of vocationalism

The above discussion covers some of the issues that emerge from a critical reading of the new Skills for Life policy. A dominant theme that emerges from my reading of various *Skills for Life* documents is a discourse of vocationalism, which defines literacy and numeracy as pre-vocational and vocationally relevant skills (see, for example, DfEE 2001b: 11). The question the critical reader will want to ask is whether literacy and numeracy aren't about more than that. Skills for Life says very little about the potential role of literacy in community participation and informed citizenship. Many researchers and adult language, literacy and numeracy practitioners criticise the vocational discourse of literacy as defining reading and writing in much too narrow terms. In their view, literacy extends beyond the utilitarian justifications for reading and writing that dominate Skills for Life.

We also need to ask how it happens that one particular concept of literacy becomes dominant. Who decides which literacy practices are included in any learning activities that are developed as part of the Skills for Life initiative? If work-related literacy and numeracy practices are the central concern of the new government policy, what happens to those learners who come to literacy classes not because they are looking for a job? The more general question is whether the vocational discourse matches the learners' own discourses? Perhaps it does for many. But it doesn't necessarily for all. What about those who join because they've always wanted to learn to write with greater confidence, or because they want to learn to read websites, so they can buy their cinema tickets online? Do such literacy practices have a place in government-financed adult LLN classes?

The Skills for Life strategy also appears to exclude (or at the very least to neglect) critical literacy (see Chapter 1). It propagates individual advancement and 'social inclusion', the aim being to help people progress within mainstream society. People do change their lives through learning and in many cases this may be primarily through individual learning, serving individual goals. On the other hand, learning – including learning literacy and numeracy – can be a tool for community action. It is striking that the government's 'success stories' of Skills for Life (see Carole Reeve) are all about individuals and their achievements. There are no accounts of how improved skills have helped communities and groups to fulfil their aims.

Many other questions regarding Skills for Life can be raised. A further question that is not addressed in any of the Skills for Life documents is what precise literacy and numeracy skills different jobs really require. Is the lack of literacy and numeracy skills the only problem that keeps people unemployed (Black 2004)? Is it not the case that, in many communities, adult language, literacy and numeracy programmes could only lead to a significant decrease in unemployment if new training facilities and new jobs were created? And what about the kinds of jobs that are available? Even if we accept that changes in the economy and the widespread use of communication technologies require more and more people to be better and better educated, there are still many low-skilled jobs without which even the most highly developed society and the most sophisticated economy cannot survive.

A related question is what do governments – when pronouncing on the need for people to improve their skills – really know about those in employment who are believed to struggle with reading and writing? How do those people manage? What strategies have they developed to deal with the literacy and numeracy requirements of their jobs? Research on workplace literacies (see, for example, Gowen 1992; Hull 1993; Black 2004) challenges the dominant discourse of literacy, numeracy and unemployment. While it does not deny that changes in the workplace have led to new skills demands, it shows that far too little is known about what workers and employers do already to adapt to these changes.

On the other hand, there are certainly many people who come to adult literacy, language and numeracy classes wishing to gain vocational skills and to improve their income. Because they lack the required basic literacy and numeracy skills, vocational training courses may not be accessible to them (Wymer 1998). It is here that Skills for Life responds to a demand whose existence few would doubt. Remember Wendy, who was introduced in Chapter 3? She spent 15 years working in social care. Wendy no longer wanted to be a carer, but because her spelling was bad and she didn't know how to work with a computer, she could not get the jobs she wanted. Her dream was to become a receptionist. For people like Wendy, the relatively formal character of adult LLN, its institutional link with further education and its focus on vocationally-relevant skills, seems to be just right.

📖 Reading

Improving Adult Basic Skills, Addressing a Generation of Neglect

(http://www.dfes.gov.uk/readwriteplus, posted 3 November 2003, accessed 26.8.04)

The first definitive national profile of adult literacy and numeracy skills was published on 30 October 2003 by the Department for Education and Skills and demonstrates the need for the Government to continue its sustained drive to improve adult basic skills training and school standards, particularly in maths.

Conducted as part of the Government's 'Skills for Life' programme to improve the literacy and numeracy skills of 1.5 million adults by 2007, the *National Needs and Impact Survey of Literacy, Numeracy and ICT Skills* assesses working adults' basic literacy and numeracy skills and shows for the first time the direct impact they have on attainment and employment prospects.

The survey demonstrates early success in the Government's drive to increase the numbers of adults with basic skills in literacy and numeracy. The proportion of adults aged 16–65 that have literacy skills below the 'Skills for Life' baseline – Level 1 (a D–G grade GCSE) – has fallen from the 7 million estimated in 1997 to 5.2 million adults now. And those that have numeracy skills below the 'Skills for Life' baseline – Entry Level 3 (the standard expected of 9–11 year olds) – has fallen slightly from the 7 million estimated in 1997 to 6.8 million adults now.

However, the survey also highlights past decades of neglect in basic skills education, revealing that 15 million adults overall lack the numeracy skills expected at a lower grade GCSE.

The survey underlines the need for the Government to continue its successful 'Skills for Life' programme, which has already seen over 1.8 million adults start basic skills courses. It also emphasises the significance of delivering the new Skills Strategy entitlement to free tuition for all those who never achieved a qualification – vocational or academic – equivalent to 5 good GCSEs or an NVQ Level 2.

And while respondents to the survey will not have benefited from recent improvements made by the introduction of literacy and numeracy strategies in primary schools or in maths attainment at secondary level, it underscores the importance of continuing to drive up school standards so that more young people are properly equipped to meet the challenge of the global economy.

The survey covered 8,730 respondents aged 16–65 years old. Key findings include:

- 1.7 million (5 per cent) of adults aged 16–65 have literacy skills below Entry Level 3 (the standard expected of 11 year olds), and 5.2 million (16 per cent) below Level 1 (less than a D–G GCSE);
- 6.8 million (21 per cent) of adults aged 16–65 have numeracy skills below Entry Level 3, and 15 million (47 per cent) below Level 1;
- men and women have similar levels of literacy, but men appear to have higher levels of numeracy, with one in three or 32 per cent of men achieving Level 2 (an A*–C GCSE) or above, compared to one in five or 19 per cent of women;
- many respondents had a high level of awareness of, and practical skills in ICT applications and terminology, with 50 per cent achieving Level 2 or above in an awareness assessment, and 47 per cent achieving Level 1 or above in a practical skills assessment;
- lower levels of literacy and numeracy were associated with socio-economic deprivation, with adults in more deprived areas tending to perform at a lower level than those in less deprived areas;
- good literacy and numeracy skills tended to be associated with good wages with 68 per cent of full-time workers with Level 2 or above in numeracy skills earning more than £20,000 a year before tax;
- parents with lower literacy and numeracy skills were less confident in helping their children with reading, writing and maths.

Publishing the survey, Minister for Skills and Vocational Education, Ivan Lewis said:

"I am determined to ensure that today's young people will no longer endure the decades of neglect in literacy and numeracy education which is reflected so starkly in this survey. Our recruitment of 50% more maths teachers in just four years and dedicated literacy and numeracy strategies in primary schools are already delivering significant improvements in maths attainment at secondary level.

"And our 'Skills for Life' programme is now giving adults the chance to get the basic skills they need to get on and succeed. In its first two years, over 1.8 million adults have started basic skills courses, and 470,000 have achieved key qualifications. We are confident of reaching our target to enable 750,000 adults to achieve a basic skills qualification by the end of 2004, and increase this to 1.5 million adults by 2007."

'Skills for Life' is just one of the measures under the Government's sustained drive to improve the nation's skills in literacy and numeracy, others include:

- the Skills Strategy, published in July, includes entitlement to free tuition for all those who never achieved a qualification – vocational or academic – equivalent to 5 good GCSEs or an NVQ Level 2. And a new Adult Learning Grant will offer £30 per week to those aged 19–30 who are studying full time for their first full qualification at level 2 or level 3;
- Literacy and Numeracy Strategies in primary schools which have led to 73 per cent of 11 year olds achieving the expected level in maths in 2003 – a 14 per cent increase since 1998;
- the post-14 Maths Inquiry set up to look at boosting the supply of people with science, technology, engineering and mathematical skills which will give a series of recommendations to Government later next month;
- the establishment of a National Centre for Excellence in Mathematics Teaching – to tackle the poor uptake of young people going into higher level maths;
- the establishment of 77 maths and computing colleges under the specialist schools programme to work with other local schools and the wider community to raise standards in numeracy;
- action to boost maths teaching and encourage more graduates to become maths teachers, with recruits to maths teaching rising by 50 per cent from 1998 to 2002.

NOTES TO EDITORS

This Press Notice applies to England.

1. The *National Needs and Impact Survey of Literacy, Numeracy and ICT Skills* is available on www.dfes.gov.uk/research The survey is based on interviews and skills assessments with 8,730 people, aged 16–65 years old, in England. The skills assessments are designed to measure the skills of the population

against the National Standards and Core Curricula for adult literacy and numeracy.

2. Previous estimates of the level of adult basic skills were published by Sir Claus Moser's working group on post-school basic skills in its report 'A Fresh Start' in 1997. Deriving figures from the International Adult Literacy Survey (IALS) and the National Child Development Study (NCDS), the report concluded that 7 million people in England had literacy skills below Level 1. For numeracy, less good data were available, and it was estimated that at least 7 million people lacked good numeracy skills, based on the number of people thought to be below Entry Level 3.

Chapter 8

Implications of the social view of literacy for the policy and practice of adult language, literacy and numeracy

What this chapter is about

In Chapter 3, I began to discuss the implications of a social view of literacy for the teaching and learning of literacy, language and numeracy. In this final chapter, I want to pursue this discussion and spend more time reflecting on what difference a social practice view of literacy (numeracy and ESOL) can make with regards to policy and practice. I start with a discussion of policy: where does the social practices view of literacy stand with regard to current adult language, literacy and numeracy policy in England and elsewhere? I ask not only how researchers from the New Literacy Studies (NLS) have reacted to the current policies (see my discussion in Chapter 7), but what they have done and can do in order to inform and influence policy.

After that, I look more specifically at practice. In doing so, I address the particular concerns of teachers and curriculum developers who want to know how a social practice view of literacy can be brought into the classroom. Albeit a relatively recent phenomenon, the NLS have not developed in isolation and there are similarities between what those adhering to a social practice view suggest and what others have been doing already. Therefore, the section on practice brings in other approaches, such as participatory education and critical literacy, to show how they relate to an NLS view of literacy. I end the chapter with a few thoughts on learning, from a social practice perspective.

One of the most innovative aspects of the NLS has been its deliberate move away from educational contexts towards everyday uses of literacy and numeracy. However, the same approach – of thinking of literacy as social practice – can and indeed should also be applied to educational contexts, such as classrooms and other places where structured instruction takes place (see Hull and Schultz 2002 for a good summary of insights from recent work in this area). Thinking of classrooms as particular social and cultural contexts helps to develop conceptual links between literacies 'outside' – that is, in 'real' life – and 'inside', meaning, within educational contexts. That the 'outside' bears upon the 'inside' – and thus should not be ignored – is one of the central arguments put forward by the NLS and thus is crucial for the discussion that follows here. To introduce this line of thought,

I begin with a brief aside on the concept of 'schooled literacy' as a way of talking about the specific practices of literacy and learning that characterise educational contexts.

Schooled ways of knowing: schooled ways of literacy

Earlier in this book, I suggested that there are multiple literacies and that these literacies are situated within particular social and cultural contexts, which shape both their form and their meaning. This is no different for reading and writing in educational contexts. A closer look at what is going on in schools or in adult language, literacy and numeracy (LLN) classes reveals a number of literacy practices that are commonly used. While some literacy practices are actively promoted through the processes of teaching and learning, others are not recognised or are even discouraged. The literacy practices of educational settings can be called 'school literacies' or 'schooled literacies' (Street 1995).

Schooled literacies have a lot to do with the objectification of written (and spoken) language. In schools and adult LLN classes, literacy is distanced from its 'real-life' social uses and turned into a set of independent and neutral skills that work according to rules, which can be taught and learned (Street 1995). The argument here is not that such skills – as, for example, the skills of coding and decoding of letters and words – are irrelevant to the processes of reading and writing. They are certainly an intrinsic part of what reading and writing is about. But literacy is about much more than the ability to employ the technology of print. Literacy is always about reading or writing something: a meaning or a message.

The purpose of literacy education should be to enable learners to 'read' these meanings, which implies the ability to read beyond and between the lines. Its purpose should also be to help them to participate meaningfully in events and activities that involve the use of written texts. However, what happens easily in the process of pedagogisation (the process of making an everyday activity, such as writing a letter, the subject of a lesson) is that literacies are being stripped of their social and ideological meanings, stripped of the purposes they serve and the activities they are part of, and as a result are treated as neutral and autonomous skills. Acquiring them can then turn into a mechanical and meaningless process of learning rules and techniques.

The idea of school literacies leads us to look at classrooms (adult LLN or school) as social and cultural institutions that have particular values and follow particular rules and procedures. Schools are associated with sitting in rows or around tables, and with or doing exercises from worksheets. Teacher-initiated question-and-answer sessions, grammar-based teaching, tests and assessments are among the dominant practices. Such school literacies typically see form as a matter of high importance. In the case of adult literacy learners, the main question is whether – or to what extent – adults need to be confined by the conventions and rules of school literacy, for example, when practising their own writing.

Literacies are closely connected to knowledge. School literacies are part and parcel of school ways of knowing. Schools value and promote academic (scientific) knowledge, rationality and mainstream cultural values and practices. The concept of school literacies is helpful, because it makes us aware of the narrow and specialised way in which current educational discourse defines reading and writing. School literacies are often treated as the only valuable form of literacy. In this view, minority and vernacular literacies do not count as valid literacy practices. This is not only the case for minority languages. In many adult LLN classes, the local experience and the vernacular literacy practices of local communities and sub-cultures are not given legitimacy. To give an example, regional dialects, such as the Scots language, are marginalised by the dominance of Standard English in the education system (Crowther and Tett 2001).

The concept of literacy that most strongly shapes current adult LLN policy in Britain is functional literacy (see Chapter 1). As with school literacy, the idea of functional literacy is part of a discourse of uniform skills and measurable levels of competence. The recent changes in adult literacy policy in England that I discussed in Chapter 6 (a national system of provision, with a national curriculum and national tests) have brought the adult language, literacy and numeracy sector closer to the conventions of formal education. As part of these changes, the language used in adult LLN has become more school-like, and typical literacy practices of schools have become more important in adult language, literacy and numeracy education (think, for example, about tests). Policies (such as Skills for Life) are designed on the basis of choices over the approach and the practices to be included. Different policies privilege different approaches and as a result different literacy practices are privileged. To give an example, in the 1970s and 1980s, student writing was an important part of adult LLN in England, but this no longer appears to be the case in the Skills for Life programme.

Policy implications: challenging dominant discourses about literacy

A socially based view of literacy provides an alternative to the functional discourse that currently dominates adult language, literacy and numeracy policy. To begin with, the social view allows us to see that there are many more literacies than the functional view acknowledges and that these literacies are central to people's lives.

The current government's commitment to adult basic education has resulted in increased provision of adult literacy, numeracy and ESOL classes. This is without doubt a positive development. From a social literacies point of view, we nevertheless have to ask what exactly these new programmes provide: what literacy practices are included in the Skills for Life strategy? Are these the dominant literacies of schools and workplaces only? And what are the values, norms and identities that are being imparted at the same time?

The social view argues that literacy programmes should do more than help people to be economically active and productive. Social literacy is about more than vocationally relevant skills and making one's contribution to the nation's economic productivity: it includes literacy for active citizenship, political participation, individual development and leisure. The purpose of literacy education that is informed by a social view is to enable learners to engage widely in activities and relationships that lie inside and outside the workplace. Furthermore, the aim is to empower adults to influence decisions that affect their lives. Here, a social practices view of literacy overlaps with the concept of critical literacy and I will come back to this later in this chapter. What is important to say at this point is that the social practice view of literacy can and should be applied to examine critically all existing literacy, numeracy and ESOL programmes (using an approach similar to the one I used in Chapter 7). Here, the NLS have an important contribution to make as an 'outside' voice that can usefully add to current policy perspectives.

One of the central implications of the social view of literacy is that adults who, according to surveys such as the IALS (see Chapter 7), are regarded as having serious literacy deficiencies, are in fact not only involved in numerous literacy and numeracy events throughout their lives, but may possess a range of informally acquired literacy and numeracy skills. The social view of literacy aims to overcome the deficit view that shapes so much of current literacy policy and practice. It asks how local, non-standard and multi-lingual literacy practices and informally acquired knowledge and skills can be validated and included in any literacy teaching. I will say more on this in the next section, which deals with practice. With regards to policy, the New Literacy Studies have an important contribution to make to current debates about 'skills'. With its ethnographic approach, the NLS are ideally placed to produce the kind of in-depth accounts of people's own literacy practices that meaningfully complement the picture derived from survey-based research. Such research can document the role of literacy and numeracy in the lives of those people at whom Skills for Life and other programmes are aimed. The justification for this is that we currently know too little about what these people do already with literacy, what skills they have, what strategies they have developed to cope, where they think they have problems and what they would like to learn.

Policy-makers may dismiss the need for such knowledge, arguing that existing surveys provide enough information on the state of literacy and numeracy in the country and that many studies have convincingly demonstrated the links between low literacy and numeracy, unemployment or underemployment, low earnings, poor health and social marginalisation. But statistics can only touch at the surface of these phenomena and they tend to isolate single factors while neglecting the complex ways in which a variety of circumstances interact with each other to produce individual situations. Statistics can tell us little about how concretely – let's say, in a group of long-term unemployed – low skills relate to their difficulties in finding a job and any other problems they may face.

Yet such information is crucial to make policies more responsive to learners' needs and aspirations. The dominant approach to policy development is on the basis of 'assumed' needs (see Castleton 2001), rather than on needs expressed by learners themselves or on an analysis of needs based on in-depth consultation and research on the ground. Knowing more about what people already do with literacy and numeracy in their lives would allow curriculum developers and teachers to develop new areas of practice that directly build on and incorporate people's existing uses of literacy and numeracy.

On a more general level, ethnographic studies of literacy have an important contribution to make to policy in that they can draw attention to the diversity of literacy in our contemporary society and challenge the dominance of standard literacies (Hamilton 2000). This includes the literacy (and numeracy) practices of non-mainstream communities and ethnic and linguistic minorities, many of which are ignored or regarded with suspicion by mainstream society and its educational institutions.

Taking account of people's own views on literacy

People with low levels of literacy not only make use of reading and writing in everyday life, but they also have views about literacy and about education generally. The term 'literacy practices' (see chapters 2 and 3) deliberately includes the uses and meanings of reading and writing, addressing people's own definitions for literacy and numeracy. Knowing about people's own discourses about literacy and numeracy helps policy-makers and planners to understand what kinds of learning programmes these people are likely to enjoy. Since the introduction of Skills for Life strategy in 2001, the government has invested heavily into its Get On campaign, a concerted effort to attract people to adult LLN classes. The enrolment figures are impressive, but some of the government's priority groups remain 'hard to reach'.

Meanwhile, the government is relentlessly pursuing its awareness-raising strategies and this begs the question how much the government understands about people's circumstances and their reasons for not joining. To say that those who do not come forward are disengaged and lack motivation – or do not recognise the problems they have – may be too easy. A social practices view of literacy suggests that we can think about non-learners in a different way. We need to find out what deters them from coming. One factor may be their negative experiences with school literacies whose predominant effect was not empowerment, but exclusion. The dominant view – that low skills cause under- or unemployment, bad health and social marginalisation – may simply not reflect their situation. Lack of literacy and numeracy, despite what the dominant discourse wants us to believe, may not be an issue for them; or they may want to do something about their skills, but may be put off by the forms of provision on offer.

The above suggests that the picture is much more complex than the public and policy-makers believe. It is true that many of those who are economically deprived, and have no access to adequate nutrition, housing, health care and education, also have little or no access to the dominant literacies of schools and workplaces. However, this does not mean that improving their reading and writing will necessarily and automatically improve their income or guarantee them access to proper housing and health care. The conditions that contribute to people's marginal position are much more complex; literacy is only one factor among many others that may be able to help them transform their lives. A social view of literacy can contribute a different way of thinking about the 'literacy problem'. What we need to do is try to steer the debate towards a view of reading and writing that does not consider literacy to be merely a matter of educational attainment alone. Rather, such a broad view sees the 'literacy problem' as related to the social and cultural exclusion that results from the current socio-economic context and from recent technological and social changes (Hamilton and Merrifield 2000).

Influencing policy: is this possible?

The above presents a number of ideas and viewpoints that are relevant for policy. Influencing policy-makers' views, however, is easier said than done. Without doubt, a lot of progress has been made in recent years in re-theorising literacy and in making the social practice approach better known. However, as Hamilton (2000: 2) remarks 'there is still a long way to go to make the NLS a credible approach within policy and practice'. A lot of work still needs to be done, undoubtedly, in bringing the approach closer to policy. Indeed, we need to do more than produce lists of suggestions, as I have done here.

What researchers can do and have tried to do is enter a dialogue with policy-makers. Active lobbying for a broader concept of literacy and a different way of thinking about the present 'literacy crisis', however, has been hindered by the entrenched ways in which the media report on the issue and the lack of co-operation between the government and research institutions. The Skills for Life programme has changed some of this and has provided new opportunities for research to inform policy. The work of the NRDC, funded by the government, has provided a new space for research on literacy, numeracy and ESOL to move into the mainstream.

There are currently several research initiatives that apply a social practice view of literacy to teaching and learning in a variety of contexts and settings (for more information on these projects, see http://www.literacy.lancs.ac.uk/ and http://www.nrdc.org.uk/). These projects focus on learners and on all those who are targeted by current policies, the aim being to understand the links between what is happening in classes and what role literacy and numeracy play in learners' lives. The dominant methodology used by researchers from Lancaster Literacy Research Centre is ethnography. This approach deliberately and purposely focuses on everyday life, while at the same time taking the ethnographic approach into the educational context.

Such work, as can be expected, is not without conflict and contradiction, and the fact that a lot of the research being carried out around Skills for Life is funded by the government creates its own ambiguities. The challenge for the researchers involved is twofold: to prove the credibility of the NLS, while not losing their original ethos and becoming co-opted by the dominant agenda of current times.

It is worth mentioning here that the NLS have been involved with policy even prior to the opening of the NRDC. However, this has mostly happened abroad. Since the mid-1990s, UK-based researchers have been involved in work supported by the Department for International Development (DfID) to promote adult literacy, language and numeracy education in the so-called developing countries. A small number of innovative projects were developed, all of which explicitly drew on the social literacies approach and sought to develop new forms of learning and teaching (see Rogers et al. 1999; Millican 2004).

As a result of these initiatives and the collaboration between researchers and DfID personnel, the notion of literacy as a social practice has found its way into the department's thinking about literacy and has helped to develop a new approach that more closely embeds adult literacy, language and numeracy teaching with other community-based and development-orientated activities. The focus of such activities is to support people in their existing uses of literacy and numeracy. I will come back to one of these initiatives in the following section, where I turn to the practice implications of the social view of literacy.

Practice implications: diversifying the currriculum and working with learners' own literacy and numeracy practices

What are the implications of the social view of literacy for the practice of adult language, literacy and numeracy teaching? How can teachers use the NLS approach to develop new ways of teaching and learning with adults? Before I respond to these questions, it is important to say that the social view of literacy did not develop in isolation, and does not see itself as opposed to all other perspectives on literacy teaching. In fact, it shares many ideas with other models of literacy, notably with participatory education and critical literacy, which is why I discuss them here.

Social views of literacy and critical literacy education

Critical literacy education is based on a belief that learning to read and write, or improving one's reading and writing, goes beyond the acquisition of new skills and includes learning 'how to use literacy to examine critically one's position in life in terms of socio-economic status, gender, educational background and race' (Degener 2001: 29). Adult literacy and numeracy programmes that are developed in a critical perspective attempt to involve students in examining the factors that determine their position in society and in developing ways to change their lives (see also Chapter 1).

Many researchers and practitioners who think of literacy as a social practice would argue that a social model of reading and writing necessarily includes a critical component. They would say that a social theory of literacy is necessarily political. The ideological model of literacy (Street 1993) invites us to examine how specific literacy practices are embedded in power structures and are used to extend institutional authority. As part of a literacy programme, learners can engage in critical discussions about the powerful literacy practices they encounter in their everyday lives, for example, bureaucratic forms (see Chapter 3). Teachers and learners together can discuss whether acquiring dominant literacy practices will really lead to the expected changes in learners' lives.

Practitioners and researchers who have sought to develop the practice implications of the social view have drawn on 'critical language awareness' (CLA) and 'critical discourse analysis' (CDA) as instruments to help learners examine particular ways of using written and spoken language (Fairclough 1992, 1995 and 2003; Chouliaraki and Fairclough 1999; Wodak and Meyer 2001). The argument is that if literacy focuses on the skills of reading and writing (and numbers) only, learners are not given any opportunity to understand how some meanings are selected and preferred, while others are not.

Jessop, Lawrence and Pitt (1998) discuss how what is called 'critical literacy practice' can be applied in adult literacy, numeracy or ESOL classes. In their work with students, they draw on CDA and CLA to critically examine a variety of texts. Developing critical language awareness means trying to understand how the particular language – written and spoken – used by institutions and public figures conveys authority and disguises ideological positions behind seemingly natural and neutral words and phrases (see Ivanič 1990; Janks and Ivanič 1992; Clark and Ivanič 1998). Such critical analysis of different literacies is an important part of literacy teaching that is grounded in a social view of literacy. This kind of teaching aims to enable learners to identify the 'meaning beyond – or between the lines – and the interests behind the meaning' (Crowther and Tett 2001: 114).

The affinities of critical and social approaches should, however, not be taken for granted. It is possible to imagine the social practice approach being tamed by a liberal agenda. To guard against this, I want to take up Shore's idea of 'critical social literacy' (2003: 20). She suggests that if we are serious about treating literacy as a social practice, this implies that we always engage with the power relations that spin around learners' own literacies. This implies going beyond the text and its readings, by examining what's being done with the text, by whom, the role it plays in institutional processes and whose purposes it serves. Ewing, reflecting on his own work as a literacy teacher in Canada, suggests that the assertions of the social practice view of literacy imply that the 'realities of communities' (Ewing 2003: 17) need to be given a central place in the literacy programme. And these, in most cases, are realities of disadvantage and disempowerment.

As an example, he refers to his own work in a neighbourhood of Toronto, where the learning of written language developed around issues of health and housing. The literacy practices that learners worked with were selected from the uses of written language in their community. Crucially, working around these practices provided space for open discussion of the issues that mattered to learners, but at the same time allowed the group to tackle the technical aspects of coding and decoding written language. Without doubt, as these and other examples show, such an integrated and critical approach to the teaching of language, literacy and numeracy can be highly stimulating and it need not descend into a liberal or even a functional approach.

Social views of literacy and participatory education

Participatory approaches to adult education have had a central place in literacy and numeracy education since the Right to Read campaign in the 1970s. The main principle of participatory adult literacy education is learner-centredness. Ideally, learners are actively involved in all stages of planning and implementation of the programme. This is most important regarding the curriculum and the expected outcomes of programmes (Auerbach 1999).

As with critical literacy education, participatory approaches have much to share with a social view of literacy. Both challenge the teacher-led and curriculum-centred ways that characterise much of current literacy education. To be participatory means to develop the curriculum based on learners' own lived realities and their own needs and aspirations. In terms of literacy practices, the implication is that literacy work starts from the purposes that literacy fulfils in learners' lives. In practice this means that learners will decide which literacies they want to be part of their learning.

If learners' everyday uses and meanings of literacy and learners' own literacy-related needs are to become the core of literacy education, we first need to find out what these literacies are. Hamilton (1999; see Reading 1, p. 141) has suggested that ethnographic research into everyday literacies – similar to the studies by researchers from the NLS – can be used as a curriculum resource. The idea is that teachers and learners engage in studying literacy practices of everyday life. An example of such work is given in Reading 2. The paper describes the experiences of a literacy group that used soap operas to discuss examples of the literacies of everyday life and the roles they played in learners' lives. This is an example of how student-led research can be used in adult language, literacy and numeracy classes.

As a teacher, you may still wonder how to make such research part of your own work. After all, ethnography is a research methodology that was developed and is mostly used by academics. In Chapter 4, I suggested that you carry out your own ethnographic study of literacy practices of your own choice. Part of the reason for doing so was to invite you to experience for yourself how the method works. Ethnography is a very flexible approach that can be used to greater or lesser degrees of intensity and depth and this helps to make it such a good tool for work with students. Furthermore, it does not rely on sophisticated research techniques.

Participant observation as a method does not require the researcher to behave in ways that are completely different to everyday normal social interaction. What it requires is a different frame of thinking, a different perspective from which to look at everyday activities. Some tools, however, are good to help get the process started. Pen and notebook are the most common ones, but more interesting perhaps is the use of cameras that allow students to take pictures of the literacy events they observe. It is also a good idea to collect literacy artefacts and to use these as a starting point for later discussions in class.

I want now to move on to the analysis of the literacy practices that students have identified and how such an analysis can be done jointly in class. To begin with, it is useful to simply list all the literacy events that students found and the texts these involved. A second step would be to identify the domains of social life these were part of. Producing such a list is likely to provoke lively debate and unexpected surprises as to the wide presence of texts in our daily lives. We live, as Dorothy Smith (1990) has suggested, in a textually mediated world. However, common notions of literacy and taken-for-granted ideas about what constitutes reading and writing (see Chapter 2) mean that many daily literacy activities are not recognised, not even by ourselves. We are not aware of the many ways in which we use texts to fulfil such mundane activities as preparing our breakfast, buying a train ticket or deciding how to spend the coming weekend.

Becoming aware of the diversity of everyday literacy practices can help learners to see their own practices in a more positive light and thereby to overcome the deficit notion that many are likely to have internalised. At a more general level, working with students' own literacy practices can pave the way towards a critical analysis of the way mainstream society and educational institutions restrict what is accepted and valued as literacy. This is particularly important when working with learners from non-mainstream backgrounds and those whose first language is not Standard English, be it working-class families from Glasgow whose home language is Scots or immigrants from West Africa whose mother tongue nobody in England has ever heard of.

Further steps in analysing the events found could follow the framework suggested in Chapter 4, looking at participants, settings, norms, behaviours and so on. When following this approach, it is a good idea for the teacher and the students to think carefully about who takes part in different literacy practices. What roles do different participants take on? Who is actively involved in the event and who is a peripheral participant or just a bystander? Whose purposes does the event serve? Who has prepared or is preparing any texts that are involved and who controls how they are read, interpreted and used? Addressing these questions can allow teachers and learners to develop a clearer picture of what actually happens in a literacy event and what precisely it is that creates difficulties for learners.

Take as an example the kind of bureaucratic forms I discussed in Chapter 3. A skills view of literacy assumes that if applicants struggle to complete the form this is because they do not understand the words used, they find the layout confusing, or they do not know how to put their answers. While I agree that all these can present difficulties, I have already suggested earlier in this book (see Chapter 3) that the reasons why people struggle are much more complex. Much has to do for example with understanding the system and procedures of which the text is part, and the nature of the applicant's rights and obligations.

Another aspect that could be brought into the discussion of learners' everyday literacies is the relationship between a text, the language it uses and the knowledge it contains. Often what results in vernacular literacies not being accepted is not only the language and style they use, but the knowledge they contain. The question not only is what do people read, but also does what they read count.

With the above, I have tried to show how research into everyday literacies can be used by learners and teachers in a variety of ways and that it can lead to a range of curriculum innovations. The ultimate purpose of this kind of work is for teachers and learners to explore ways to re-examine and re-value their own literacy practices and to create a space within the educational context for these literacies and for the knowledge they contain. The ethnographic approach of the NLS is a particularly suitable tool to unpack what is happening in literacy events and to understand what roles different people take in it. One particular suggestion that has derived from the social practice view of literacy is the use of 'real literacy texts' such as letters, invoices or forms (see Rogers et al. 1999). Rather than using these for the teaching of coding and decoding skills, the idea would be to make these part of the kind of critical analysis I suggested above.

Another option is to integrate the teaching of reading and writing with the activities of community groups and thereby to dispense with 'isolated' literacy or numeracy classes. This approach, which has affinities with current work in England on 'embedded' literacy and numeracy provision, was tried out in an innovative project in Nepal. The Community Literacy Project in Nepal (CLPN; see their website at http://www.clpn.org) was developed with the explicit aim of using the concept of literacy as a social practice. The project, which was supported by the British Department for International Development (DfID), used ethnographic studies of community literacy practices as the basis for developing the curriculum. From this, a range of activities were set up with the aim of helping communities to broaden their engagement with literacy practices and use these for their own purposes and desires.

On learning

The attentive reader will not have failed to notice that although much of this book has been concerned with the uses of reading and writing in everyday life, and with the politics and practices of teaching adults to improve their reading and writing, I have said very little about learning. What has been missing is a discussion of what a social practice approach to literacy (and numeracy) means in terms of learning. The skills view of literacy has a clear idea of what the learning of literacy is about: it means learning to code and decode letters, words and sentences, learning the rules of grammar and spelling, and so on. But how does the social practice view of literacy conceptualise learning? How do we describe what learning is? Keeping in line with the NLS focus on everyday life, the central question is: how do adults learn literacy in everyday life?

To be frank, the social practice view of literacy has not yet developed a theory of learning that would fit its understanding of literacy as social practice, although some work has been done recently (see, for example, Gee 2004). This is not to say that researchers in the NLS have no interest in learning and that they have not studied how people learn. Many of the ethnographies of literacy that are published contain data on learning. However, the insights to be gained from these have not yet been put together in any systematic way.

In their book *Local Literacies*, Barton and Hamilton (1998) describe the lives of several individuals who entered new spheres of activities, became part of new groups and networks and engaged in new activities. These new activities resulted from changes in their life circumstances – a divorce, a move to a new town or district, an illness or financial difficulty. Strikingly, such changes required people to develop new forms of expertise and to engage with new literacy practices. And they triggered people's interest in learning.

When her son was diagnosed as dyslexic, Shirley, one of Barton and Hamilton's informants, began to read books and magazine articles about dyslexia. When she became the editor of the local residents' association, she learned how to write editorials. Cliff, another of Barton and Hamilton's informants, used literacy to increase his knowledge about tinnitus, a condition he suffered from. For example, he read medical charts about hearing tests. At some point in his life, Harry, whom you may remember from Chapter 2, began to write his own book about his wartime experiences. Becoming a writer had been a gradual process for him, from carefully drafted letters to his first story (which he asked his son 'to flower up') and finally to the book. In the process, Harry learned new literacy practices.

Examples such as these suggest that learning could be conceptualised in the following way. First of all, learning entails a change in a person's ability to participate in a literacy event. By this I mean, for example, a move from being a peripheral participant who has little control over the event and little ability to use it for their own ends, to becoming a more central, more active agent in the event. And this includes using literacy, using text in this context in a way that satisfies the learner's own desires and needs. It also involves learning the discourses that shape the particular practice and becoming a member of a new discourse community (see Barton 1994).

Literacy is often a key instrument in access to and benefit from knowledge and from services and this requires people to engage with institutions and settings they may not be familiar with (Hamilton 2000). The ability to control the literacy events that are part of such encounters can be crucial to making these encounters meaningful and successful in the eyes of the user. In these contexts, learning takes place in the way suggested above, by moving from a marginal position to being centrally involved in the literacy event and in control of it.

Secondly, learning could mean expanding one's own literacy repertoire, engaging with new forms of texts, discovering new ways of writing, exploring new ways of using print for various activities. In a recent paper, Ewing (2003) suggests that adult literacy learners develop their own strategies to make meaning from literacies that extend beyond their current abilities to process written language. This happens in classrooms, as part of structured teaching and learning. But the same happens in everyday life and it is a phenomenon not limited to the uneducated.

Another issue that emerges from existing studies of literacy in everyday life is the collaborative nature of much reading and writing, and much learning of new literacies. It is reasonable to assume that in everyday life we not only use literacy together but we also learn new literacies collaboratively. If learning in 'real life' is often collaborative, how does that fit with the more individual approach taken in many adult language, literacy and numeracy programmes? A further question concerns assessment. If learning means expanding one's own literacy repertoire and/or becoming a more active participant in literacy events, how can such learning be measured? The tests currently used in England are unlikely to capture such changes.

A final point that I would like to make is that, in settings where new powerful literacies were brought in from outside and imposed on people, researchers found that those at the recipient end did not passively accept these, but actively 'took hold' of them (Kulick and Stroud 1993). In the process they appropriated new literacies for their own purposes and incorporated them into their own cultural ways of knowing and communicating. This, in my view, is an important point to end on: adults are not passive; their learning is a process of actively engaging with new ideas and new techniques. Expanding one's own literacy repertoire always entails an element of transformation – at the end of which neither the learners' old practices nor the new ones they have absorbed remain completely the same.

Summary and conclusions

In this final chapter, I have discussed the policy and practice implications that derive from a social practice view of literacy. Some of these suggestions, such as the idea of asking learners to research their own literacy practices, have already been successfully implemented by adult LLN teachers. Several literacy projects exist that have developed detailed strategies to work with a social model of literacy, and the experiences of these initiatives have helped to further develop the practical side of the NLS.

Much more needs to be done, however, to develop workable models and strategies of how to use the social practice model for teaching. One area that requires more attention is notions of learning in everyday life and how everyday strategies of learning can be taken into educational settings. Much more also needs to be done in terms of carrying forward a dialogue between policy, practice and research with regard to the role the NLS can play in the current climate of adult language, literacy and numeracy. The challenge for the NLS is on the one hand to engage more directly with policy-makers' concerns (for example their focus on vocational skills), while on the other hand not to lose sight of the learners, and their priorities and perspectives.

📖   *Reading 1*

Hamilton, M. (1999) 'Ethnography for classrooms: constructing a reflective curriculum for literacy', *Curriculum Inquiry*, pp. 437–439.

In this short extract from a paper by Mary Hamilton, she discusses the role of ethnography as a curriculum resource for literacy teaching. Hamilton suggests that ethnography 'has potential as a learning resource, encouraging reflection, and theorising about literacy and critical engagement with questions about what literacy really is: how it is changing; how it is distributed around our neighbourhoods and communities; how we do it; and, perhaps, most importantly of all, what it is for' (pp. 430–431).

Practical Examples of Ethnography for the Literacy Classroom

I have argued above that ethnography is about self-reflection, and observing closely the everyday practices going on around us. It is a stance from which the world is viewed, as much as a method or technique. It can be doing research focused on everyday practices, either inside or outside of the classroom. It can also be used as a method of professional development. This section offers a variety of examples where people have creatively merged the boundaries between research, teaching and learning.

The first set of examples is concerned with research on everyday practices in local communities outside of formal educational settings. This research involves close observation, detailed interviewing and analysis of texts, and is carried out in the form of ethnographic work in specific, bounded communities. There is a growing body of such data now within the UK: my own work has been the Literacy in the Community study (see Barton & Hamilton, 1998). In this we have been documenting the reading and writing which people do in their everyday lives in Lancaster, England, including what goes on in people's homes and how this is different from the media stereotypes.

The sense of there being different literacies is very clear in multilingual communities where different literacy practices can be associated with different languages (see for example, Hodge & Jones (1996, working in Blackburn and in North Wales), Bhatt (1995, working in Leicester) and Saxena (1994, in London). Eve Gregory is currently looking at roles of siblings in supporting literacy learning in the Bangladeshi community in East London (Gregory, 1998, 1999). Gemma Moss, who is working in primary school classrooms to explore how gender differences in literacy learning emerge, has given the children cameras which they use to take pictures of their home environment for later discussion.

A further set of examples come from institutional contexts which are neither everyday nor educational in the traditional sense of the term. For example, Anita Wilson has carried out a detailed ethnographic study of prison literacy (Wilson, 1996). This is an institutional setting where there are extremely strong public stereotypes of illiteracy and of problems with reading and writing. To take one example, she has investigated the amount of letter writing that goes on. Away from the education wing of prisons and within a group that you would expect using little reading and writing – young males – there is a tremendous amount of letter writing and it has great social significance.

Working in a therapeutic setting Susie Parr has adapted an ethnographic approach in her work with stroke patients suffering from aphasia who typically lose many of their literacy skills (Parr, 1995). She describes her dissatisfaction with the assessment methods traditionally available – functional assessments based on a fixed list of tasks and skills, and cognitive neuropsychological assessments that led to overly mechanistic and reductionist therapies. She set about interviewing aphasic patients about how their literacy practices had changed as a result of their stroke, about their strategies for coping with these changes and how they perceived their situation. She found that people respond in a variety of ways to the loss of previous skills, developing complex support and back-up systems with the help of friends and family, and not always wanting to regain previous levels of literacy skill, preferring to withdraw from certain roles or move into different areas of activity. These responses were key to deciding what kind of therapeutic programme would be appropriate for a given person.

The third example is a different kind of approach, inspired by ideas from community writing and publishing. The Workplace Basic Skills project organised by Fiona Frank has set up residential weekends which bring together participants to compare their practices in the workplace, and the role of literacy and basic skills courses in their working lives, and how these relate to changing technologies and practices in the workplace. Participants from a range of different workplaces have been offered the opportunity to research and document their experiences with this particular focus in mind (see Frank, 1992).

The translation of such research into educational settings is just a small step. As an example within adult education, Nora Hughes, who was a member of the Diploma in Literacy course at Goldsmiths College, London took Mukul Saxena's (1994) description of the literacy practices of members of a multilingual Punjabi community in Southall and used it to design a set of activities for her ESOL classes, transforming her students into ethnographers, researching their own communities and generating new curriculum materials and methods in the process (Hughes, 1992).

A second example is the 'Connect' Family literacy project in Lothian in which teachers and parents co-research home practices and use the information to inform curricula for family literacy courses (see Keen, 1995). In this case, a clearly thought through stance on family literacy drew on Elsa Auerbach's (1989) discussion of the relationship between home and school in family literacy programmes in the USA, and has led to a practical strategy. Activities involve interviews, parents keeping literacy diaries and 'local investigations' that document the ways the reading and writing are used in the local community, including the variety of print that can be seen around the environment in which people conduct their lives. Roz Ivanič at Lancaster is currently engaged in co-research between primary school teachers and parents of children at Key Stage 2, to explore the ways in which children carrying out school projects, draw on the resources of home and neighbourhood.

Research

In Chapter 4, I invited you to carry out your own study of everyday literacies. What did you learn from this exercise about the nature of literacy and numeracy in everyday life? What do your findings reveal of the social and situated nature of literacy and numeracy practices?

Now think about how you carried out the study and discuss whether a similar exercise could be used with students in an adult literacy, numeracy or ESOL class. How could you, as Hamilton suggests, use such studies as a curriculum resource?

📖 *Reading 2*

Roberts, G. and Prowse, J. (1999) 'Reporting soaps', *RaPAL Bulletin* 38: 26–29.

Gary Roberts and Jane Prowse are Community Education Workers who were lucky enough to be working for Connect at the time the events described in this article took place. They are both 'adult returners'. Gary is now based in Gracemount High School, Edinburgh, focusing on family literacy, where Jane also works part time.

We came to Sheffield with this research because we wanted to show that research can be fun in spite of practical limitations (money and time). We wanted to share practice and the educational opportunities of co-research and to enthuse others with the research 'bug'.

By October 1997 soaps had become 'a sexy educational issue' and we had already used them. This article is the report of the soap research carried out by the Family Literacy Project, known as Connect, based in the Pilton (of *Trainspotting* fame) area of Edinburgh. The project, in January 1997, unwittingly, pre-empted the Government's employment of soap operas and used the medium as a basis for investigating literacy events and practices.[1]

---

1 Ivanič, Barton (eds), Writing in the community (London: Sage, 1991).

The catalyst for the use of soap operas in the research came about because 'soaps' were talked about at length before many group sessions started and several parent/carers bought magazines which gave the story-lines for the next few months. Parents/carers would express opinions about how good or bad the story-line was especially if it involved a 'life issue' that had relevance to the groups.

It became apparent that the majority of family literacy groups were interested in and regularly followed soap opera story-lines. Connect staff believed that this interest and knowledge of soap operas could be built on and used as the starting point for an investigation into literacy events and practices because the majority of soaps tend to focus more on the home and community domains. This, it was felt, would allow an opportunity to critically analyse traditional 'school literacy' and the values placed on it.

In addition, the co-researchers would be put in the position of 'expert', whereby their opinion was accepted as knowledgeable, valued and enabled them to take up ownership of the research.

The co-researchers (parent/carers) were asked to watch and record the literacy *events* they observed in a soap opera of their choice and collect any newspaper or magazine articles about that soap during the 'watching' period. These findings would then be used to create a checklist of the 'soap' *events* identified together with frequency of their use. The checklist would then be utilised as a 'tool' to identify the *events* in the homes and community of Pilton. This would then allow a comparison between the already established media portrayal of literacy *events* with the every day *events* and *practices* of the co-researchers.

One of the existing Connect groups decided to develop their checklist for the research component of 'An Introduction to People & Society' a Scotvec Module that they were studying for at the time.

The total number of co-researchers involved in 'watching' the soaps for literacy events, practices and frequency was fifty-three. Of these twenty-seven continued with the research and completed the identification of their home and community literacy *events* and *practices*. These co-researchers were members of the three existing, two new and one non-Connect group.

Results from the soaps were both interesting and informative. It became apparent from the figures collated that as the co-researchers progressed from soap watching to look at *events* in their own homes and community lives, they became more aware of the many literacies they practised and how these are inter-related. (This could be because the primary focus of the research was on their own *events* and *practices* or because of the way non-school literacy is portrayed by soaps).

This can be evidenced by the doubling of noted literacy *events* recognised by the co-researchers in their homes as compared to those identified in the 'soap' home. The most frequently noted literacy *event* was reading the newspaper. This evidences the value that the co-researchers place on 'non-book' literacy and how their understanding of 'different' literacies had evolved. If newspapers do play such an integral part in Pilton life then further research into what and how this form of the media could be utilised could be very useful to schools, especially in the way they communicate with parents.

The diversity of *events* was much wider in all Pilton findings. There were also several interesting literacy *events* identified in the soaps e.g. the use of bleepers which led to a discussion about the numeracy and reading involved in their use. "Choosing horses for the Derby", was considered very much a home activity, and using "a Bookies" the community follow-on *event*.

Interesting to many of the co-researchers was identification of 'oral literacy', or as one co-researcher referred to as 'just talking'. This 'discovery' was considered by the co-researchers important and was first identified by a group who were discussing events shown in 'The Bill' where tape recordings of witnesses being interviewed were later transcribed. The co-researchers understanding of 'oral literacy' developed as their research progressed to identify that soap operas themselves are scripted pieces of work.

The buying of Lottery tickets, scratch cards, and the reading of weekly winning numbers in outlets (local shops) has impacted on *events* and practices since its inception three years ago. Over three quarters of the co-researchers associated *events* relating to these lottery activities.

A long list of literacy *events* involved in the domestic life of cooking, cleaning and child rearing were generated by the findings: these included the more obvious examples of reading and writing recipes to the reading and numeracy involved in using appliances, reading/checking meters and using cooking equipment.

One of the non-Connect group members produced his own survey of literacy events seen or heard on a variety of TV and radio programmes from the News at 10 to Masters Snooker. He was so disappointed by the lack of what he described as 'representative literacy' that he requested the research project write a letter of complaint to the BBC and ITV companies about the poor example they were giving!

All these events identified by the co-researchers show how the research process encouraged the recognition of different 'literacies' but more importantly, generated discussion within the groups about these 'different literacies'.

The co-researchers from the non-Connect group initially experienced problems with the term 'anything to do with literacy'. They had been asked, like all other participating groups, to watch and note 'anything to do with reading, writing or number' and from this they took the meaning to be 'looking for signs of illiteracy'. They expressed the view that "at their age they were not involved in education". In spite of the fact some had grandchildren who were at nursery/school and they themselves attended a class at their local community high school. They concluded that they "could be of no help to Connect as a group because some of them did not watch soaps".

Overall this research enabled the co-researchers to identify their home, school, community literacies and frequencies. It allowed them to begin to value these literacies while critically challenging their understanding of literacy in society. Finally it allowed the project to develop a responsive curriculum that built on these home and community literacies and new ways of discussing them. Thanks must be given to the co-researchers for participating, without them there would have been nothing to write about and for Jim Crowther (Moray House, Edinburgh) for his theoretical expertise.

Reflection

Reading 2 describes an exercise in researching students' own literacy practices. In this case, it seems that research into students' own literacies led to useful and important discussions in the group. The authors claim that this helped students to begin to value their own literacies. But can this be achieved so easily, if in public life and work certain literacies – different from people's own literacies – dominate?

Additional reading

Crowther, J. and Tett, L. (2001) 'Democracy as a way of life: literacy for citizenship', in J. Crowther, M. Hamilton and L. Tett (eds) *Powerful Literacies*, Leicester: NIACE, pp. 108–121.
Street, B.V. (1997) 'The implications of the "New Literacy Studies" for literacy education', *English in Education* 31 (3): 45–59.

Conclusions

With this book, I have tried to achieve two purposes: first, to introduce readers to a social practice view of literacy and its implications for the policy and practice of adult language, literacy and numeracy (LLN) and, second, to offer a critical discussion of current adult LLN policies in Britain and elsewhere.

The principal argument that I put forward in this book is that literacy is more than an abstract set of skills. It is more appropriate to think about literacy as social and situated practice. It is social, because reading and writing always involve people communicating and interacting with each other. It is social also because literacy is part of what determines relationships between people. Literacy is situated, because it is always embedded in a broader social practice and, within it, literacy itself is bound to other structures and institutions. The above also suggests that literacy is cultural, and when we speak about literacy as social practice we commonly imply this to include the 'cultural', that is, the values, ideas, conventions, identities and worldviews that shape the event of which literacy is part.

If literacy is not just a skill, but a social practice, this has important implications for how we study reading and writing, and how we learn and teach new literacies. Part of this book was devoted to exploring these new ways of studying literacy and as the reader you may have spent some time exploring for yourself what it means to carry out a study of literacy in everyday life. In the process, you may have reviewed some of your own literacy practices, or you may have examined with a fresh perspective the literacy practices of others, perhaps including those commonly labelled as lacking basic reading and writing skills. In a further step, I suggested ways of using the same ethnographic approach both to inform policy as well as to develop activities that can be carried out with literacy learners. With regard to policy, ethnography can provide detailed pictures of the role of literacy in learners' lives. Such ethnographies can go a long way in refuting the deficit views that underline current policy discourses about literacy and in making policy-makers aware of learners' 'real' needs. As for practice, I illustrated how ethnography can be used as a curriculum resource, getting students involved in researching their own literacy (numeracy and language) practices and helping to stimulate discussion and reflection on the various practices that are important to them and that they may want to acquire.

Throughout the book, I have tried to keep an eye on issues of power in relation to literacy (numeracy and ESOL): who possesses what literacies and what do these allow people to do; who is excluded from which literacies and how do particular literacy practices (e.g., certain institutional practices) disempower some and privilege others. I have also asked how certain discourses about literacy (and numeracy and ESOL) have become prominent in policy and have dominated the agenda of governments and education providers. In regard to current policy, I raised questions about the status of people's own literacy and language practices in the curriculum and the assumptions Skills for Life makes about which literacy practices students most urgently want to acquire. A further issue I raised is to what extent the new curricula take into account students' own ways of learning and their own ways of knowing (a point that may be particularly important for ESOL learners).

In Chapter 8, I suggested that as researchers and practitioners we need to pursue a critical social approach to literacy, numeracy and ESOL and I pointed out ways we can apply this perspective. The question that remains is how realistic it is to believe in the possibilities for such work to be done, given the narrow terms of the current policy framework. The aim of current literacy policy in England appears to be to create a skilled workforce rather than an informed and active citizenry (Hamilton and Merrifield 2000). If this is so, is there space for a critical social approach? And, in promoting such an approach, are we not pursuing a romantic ideal?

Critics of the social practice view of literacy (see McCabe 1998) accuse it of promoting vernacular literacies that in the current climate are irrelevant to people's position in the world. They argue that to promote vernacular literacies means that as educators we perpetuate learners' exclusion from the dominant literacy practice they desire to access. Much can be said in response to this accusation and I want to make a few points here. Firstly, promoting vernacular literacies does not equal denying people access to the powerful literacies of workplaces and public institutions. Secondly, encouraging critical reflection on people's own literacy practices does not mean a descent into romanticism. The critical approach implies that all practices – including one's own – need to be examined. Finally, and perhaps most importantly, the above criticism emanates from the view that access to the dominant literacy practices of formal institutions and workplaces is the only goal of adult LLN. A critical social approach to adult LLN does not share this view. Access to dominant literacies is crucial and it would be wrong to deny learners such access. But it perpetuates the status quo.

Ultimately, the goal of a critical social approach is to challenge the current configuration of dominant and marginal literacies. Languages are changing and so are literacies and our current world is full of examples of these changing language and literacy practices – from new e-literacies and 'textese', to experimental forms of writing and new creoles, to new multimodal forms of expression. Where does school literacy stand in relation to all these literacies? How can those who promote the 'standard' continue to ignore the fact that what is 'really useful literacy' (Martin and Rahman 2001) can only be decided by individuals and communities themselves?

The dominant discourse of work and skills not only remains powerful, but it is also strikingly narrow. With regard to workplace literacies in particular, one wonders whether the dominant discourse of human resource development has acknowledged that what are 'marketable' skills is itself subject to continuous change and diversification. To give an example, what many may regard as the playful and pointless games of teenage online surfing and video gaming are in fact highly likely to equip these youngsters with skills and experiences that many employers are looking to find amongst their staff (Merchant 2001). And yet, we are being told over and over again that as workers and employees we need to train and retrain, in order to keep up with the changing nature of work, to be efficient and competitive. How much do policy-makers know about the many highly useful and relevant literacy skills that people acquire through their own self-controlled literacy practices?

Within the discourse of the knowledge economy and its 'new work order' (Gee, Hull and Lanksheer 1996), lack of literacy and numeracy is a dark spot that governments are eager to erase. Many of the recent policy developments in adult literacy, numeracy and ESOL, as I have argued in this book, are motivated by this desire. Hence the dominance of the vocational agenda over older, more liberal or more critical models of adult LLN. But despite the hegemony of economic concerns, what content and what values dominate adult LLN in England is still a matter of debate. There are still adult literacy initiatives in the UK that explicitly pursue a broad humanistic and a politically informed agenda. Such initiatives are informed by critical and social views of literacy.

A social practice approach to literacy has much to contribute to such initiatives and it can support the work of all those who aim towards challenging and reversing the dominant understandings of what counts as useful literacy and the narrow terms under which the debates around the 'literacy crisis' is being construed. The goal of such endeavours is to bring to the fore new 'powerful' literacies, be they the marginalised literacies of working class communities in the North-West of England or the literacy practices of immigrants from Somali. The agenda for promoting such literacies, as Crowther, Hamilton and Tett (2001:3) point out, 'has to be informed by issues of social justice, equality and democracy in everyday life' thereby locating literacy within the struggles for active citizenship, social inclusion (in a broad sense) and cultural diversity, rather than treating it abstractly as an issue of skills and individual competence.

References

Chapter I

Ball, S. (1990) 'Introducing Monsieur Foucault', in S. Ball (ed.) *Foucault and Education. Disciplines and Knowledge*, London and New York: Routledge.

Barton, D. (1994) *Literacy – An Introduction to the Ecology of Written Language*, London: Blackwell.

Baynham, M. (1995) *Literacy Practices*, London and New York: Longman.

Bhola, H.S. (1994) *A Sourcebook for Literacy*, Paris: UNESCO.

DfEE (1999) *A Fresh Start: The Report of a Working Group Chaired by Sir Claus Moser*, London: Department for Education and Employment.

DfEE (2001a) *Skills for Life: The National Strategy for Improving Adult Literacy and Numeracy Skills*, Nottingham: DfEE Publications.

Fairclough, N. (2003) *Analysing Discourse: Textual Analysis for Social Research*, London: Routledge.

Foucault, M. (1980) *Power/ Knowledge. Selected Interviews and Other Writings, 1972–1977*, edited by C. Gordon, New York and London: Prentice Hall.

Freire, P. (1972) *Pedagogy of the Oppressed*, London: Penguin.

Freire, P. and Macedo, D. (1987) *Literacy: Reading the Word and the World*, South Hadley, Massachusetts: Bergin & Garvey.

Gee, J.P. (1996) *Social Linguistics and Literacies*, 2nd edn, London: Taylor & Francis.

Gee, J.P. (1999) *An Introduction to Discourse Analysis*, London and New York: Routledge.

Gray, W.S. (1956) *The Teaching of Reading and Writing*, Paris: UNESCO.

Lister, I. (1994) 'Conscientization and political literacy: a British encounter with Paulo Freire', in P. McLaren and C. Lankshear (eds) *Politics of Liberation. Paths from Freire*, London: Routledge.

OECD (1995) *Literacy, Economy and Society: Results of the First International Literacy Survey*, Paris: OECD.

OECD/CERI (1997) *Education Policy Analysis*, Paris: OECD.

OECD (2000) *Literacy in the Information Age*, Paris: OECD.

Rassool, N. (1999) *Literacy for Sustainable Development in the Age of Information*, Clevedon: Multilingual Matters.

Searle, J. (1999) *Discourses of Literacy*, Queensland: Language Australia.

Shor, I. (1993) 'Education is politics: Paulo Freire's critical pedagogy', in P. McLaren and P. Leonard (eds) *Paulo Freire. A Critical Encounter*, London: Routledge.

Street, B.V. (1993) 'Introduction: The New Literacy Studies', in B.V. Street (ed.) *Cross-Cultural Approaches to Literacy*, Cambridge: CUP.

Street, B.V. (1999) 'The meanings of literacy', in D.A. Wagner, R.L. Venetzky and B.V. Street (eds) *Literacy: An International Handbook*, Boulder, Colorado: Westview Press.

Chapter 2

Ahern, L. (2001) *Invitations to Love. Literacy, Love Letters and Social Change in Nepal*. Ann Arbor: University of Michigan Press.

Barton, D. (1994) *Literacy – The Ecology of Written Language*, London: Blackwell.

Barton, D. and Hamilton, M. (1998) *Local Literacies: Reading and Writing in One Community*, London: Routledge.

Barton, D. and Hamilton, M. (2000) 'Literacy practices', in D. Barton, M. Hamilton and R. Ivanič (eds) *Situated Literacies: Reading and Writing in Context*, London and New York: Routledge.

Barton, D., Hamilton, M. and Ivanič, R. (eds) (2000) *Situated Literacies: Reading and Writing in Context*, London and New York: Routledge.

Barton, D. and Ivanič, R. (eds) (1991) *Writing in the Community*, London: Sage.

Baynham, M. and Baker, D. (2002) '"Practice" in literacy and numeracy research: multiple perspectives", *Ways of Knowing*, 2: 1–9.

Besnier, N. (1995) *Literacy, Emotion and Authority: Reading and Writing on a Polynesian Atoll*, New York: CUP.

Bialostok, S. (2002) 'Metaphors for literacy: a cultural model of white middle-class parents', *Linguistics and Education*, 13 (3): 347–371.

Collins, J. and Blot, R.K. (2003) *Literacy and Literacies*, Cambridge: CUP.

Fairclough, N. (2003) *Analysing Discourse: Textual Analysis for Social Research*, London: Routledge.

Gee, J.P. (1996) *Social Linguistics and Literacies*, 2nd edn, London: Taylor & Francis.

Goody, J. (ed.) (1968) *Literacy in Traditional Societies*, Cambridge: CUP.

Goody, J. (1986) *The Logic of Writing and the Organisation of Society*, Cambridge: CUP.

Hamilton, M. (2000) 'Expanding the New Literacy Studies: Using photographs to explore literacy as social practice', in D. Barton, M. Hamilton and R. Ivanič (eds) *Situated Literacies. Reading and Writing in Context*, London: Routledge.

Heath, S.B. (1983) *Ways with Words*, Cambridge: CUP.

Johnston, B. (1999) 'Adult numeracy', in D. Wagner, R.L. Venetzky and B.V. Street (eds) *Literacy: An International Handbook*, Boulder, Colorado: Westview Press.

Kulick, D. and Stroud, C. (1993) 'Conceptions and uses of literacy in a Papua New Guinean village' in B.V. Street (ed.) *Cross-Cultural Approaches to Literacy*, Cambridge: CUP.

Maddox, B. (2001) 'Literacy and the market: the economic uses of literacy among the peasantry in north-west Bangladesh', in B.V. Street (ed.) *Literacy and Development: Ethnographic Perspectives*, London: Routledge.

Martin-Jones, M. and Jones, K. (eds) (2000) *Multilingual Literacies. Reading and Writing Different Worlds*, Amsterdam and Philadelphia: John Benjamins.

McCabe, C. (1998) 'A response to Brian Street', *English in Education*, 32/1: 26–28.

Olson, D. (1977) 'From utterance to text: the bias of language in speech and writing', *Harvard Educational Review*, 47: 257–281.

Olson, D. (1994) *The World on Paper*, Cambridge: CUP.

Rassool, N. (1999) *Literacy for Sustainable Development in the Age of Information*, Clevedon: Multilingual Matters.

Rogers, A., Maddox, B., Millican, J., Newell Jones, K., Papen, U. and Robinson-Pant, A.

(1999) *Re-defining Post-literacy in a Changing World*, London: Department for International Development, Education Research, Serial No. 29.

Scribner, S. and Cole, M. (1981) *The Psychology of Literacy*, Cambridge, MA: Harvard University Press.

Street, B.V. (1984) *Literacy in Theory and Practice*. Cambridge: CUP.

Street, B.V. (ed.) (1993) *Cross-Cultural Approaches to Literacy*, Cambridge: CUP.

Street, B.V. (1997) 'The implications of the "New Literacy Studies" for literacy education', *English in Education*, 31/3: 45–59.

Street, B.V. (2000) 'Literacy "events" and literacy "practices": theory and practice in the "New Literacy Studies"', in K. Jones and M. Martin-Jones (eds) *Multilingual Literacies. Reading and Writing Different Worlds*, Amsterdam and Philadelphia: John Benjamins.

Tusting, K. and Barton, D. (forthcoming) 'Community-based local literacies research', in R. Beach, J. Green, M. Kamil and T. Shanhan (eds) *Multidisciplinary Perspectives on Literacy Research*, Cresskill, New Jersey: Hampton Press.

Chapter 3

Barton, D. (1994) *Literacy – The Ecology of Written Language*, London: Blackwell.

Barton, D. and Hamilton, M. (1998) *Local Literacies*, London: Routledge.

Barton, D. and Hamilton, M. (2000) 'Literacy practices', in D. Barton, M. Hamilton and R. Ivanič (eds) *Situated Literacies: Reading and Writing in Context*, London and New York: Routledge.

Baynham, M. and Lobanga Masing, H. (2000) 'Mediators and mediation in multilingual literacy events', in M. Martin-Jones and K. Jones (eds) *Multilingual Literacies*, Amsterdam: John Benjamins.

Brandt, D. and Clinton, K. (2002) 'Limits of the local: expanding perspectives on literacy as a social practice', *Journal of Literacy Research*, 34 (3): 337–356.

Camitta, M. (1993) 'Vernacular writing: varieties of literacy among Philadelphia high school students', in B.V. Street (ed.) *Cross-cultural Approaches to Literacy*, Cambridge: CUP, pp. 228–246.

Fairclough, N. (2001) *Language and Power*, 2nd edn, London: Longman.

Fawns, M. and Ivanič, R. (2001) 'Form-filling as a social practice: taking power into our own hands', in J. Crowther, M. Hamilton and L. Tett (eds) *Powerful Literacies*, Leicester: NIACE.

Frank, F. (2001) 'Empowering literacy learners and teachers: the challenge of information and communication technology (ICT)', in J. Crowther, M. Hamilton and L. Tett (eds) *Powerful Literacies*, Leicester: NIACE.

Freebody, P. and Freiberg, J. (1999) 'Health literacy and social practice: response to Nutbeam', *Literacy and Numeracy Studies* 9 (2): 57–66.

Jones, C., Turner, J. and Street, B.V. (eds) (1999) *Student Writing in the University*, Amsterdam: John Benjamins.

Jones, K. (2000a) 'Texts, mediation and social relations in a bureaucratised world', in M. Martin-Jones and K. Jones (eds) *Multilingual Literacies*, Amsterdam: John Benjamins, pp. 209–229.

Jones, K. (2000b) 'Becoming just another alphanumerical code: farmers' encounters with the literacy and discourse practices of agricultural bureaucracy at the livestock auction', in D. Barton, M. Hamilton and R. Ivanič (eds) *Situated Literacies*, London: Routledge.

Kalman, J. (1999) *Writing on the Plaza*, Cresskill, NJ: Hampton Press.

Lea, M. and Stierer, B. (eds) (2000) *Student Writing in Higher Education*, Buckingham: Open University Press.

Lillis, T. (2001) *Student Writing*, London: Routledge.

Martin-Jones, M. and Jones, K. (eds) (2000) *Multilingual Literacies*, Amsterdam: John Benjamins.

Prinsloo, M. and Breier, M. (eds) (1996) *The Social Uses of Literacy*, Amsterdam: John Benjamins.

Rockhill, K. (1993) 'Gender, language and the politics of literacy', in B.V. Street (ed.) *Cross-cultural Approaches to Literacy*, Cambridge: CUP, pp. 156–176.

Saxena, M. (1993) 'Literacies among the Panjabis in Southall (Britain)', in J. Maybin (ed.) *Language and Literacy in Social Practice*, Clevedon: Multilingual Matters/The Open University.

Street, B.V. (1993) 'Introduction: the New Literacy Studies', in B.V. Street (ed.) *Cross-Cultural Approaches to Literacy*, Cambridge: CUP.

Street, B.V. (2001) 'Introduction', in B.V. Street (ed.) *Literacy and Development: Ethnographic Perspectives*, London: Routledge.

Street, B.V and Street, J. (1995) 'The schooling of literacy', in B.V. Street (ed.) *Social Literacies*, London: Longman.

Chapter 4

Barton, D. and Hamilton, M. (1998) *Local Literacies*, London: Routledge.

Barton, D., Hamilton, M. and Ivanič, R. (eds) (2000) *Situated Literacies: Reading and Writing in Context*, London and New York: Routledge.

Clifford, J. (1986) 'Introduction: partial truths', in J. Clifford and G.E. Marcus (eds) (1986) *Writing Culture: The Politics and Poetics of Ethnography*, Berkeley and Los Angeles: University of California Press.

Davies, C.A. (1999) *Reflexive Ethnography*, London: Routledge.

Hall, S. (ed.) (1997) *Representation: Cultural Representations and Signifying Practices*, London: Sage.

Kell, C. (1996) 'Literacy practices in an informal settlement in the Cape Peninsula', in M. Prinsloo and M. Breier (eds) *The Social Uses of Literacy. Theory and Practice in Contemporary South Africa*, Amsterdam: John Benjamins.

Malinowski, B. (1922) *Argonauts of the Western Pacific*, London: Routledge. (See in particular the Introduction, in which he sets out his principles of ethnographic fieldwork.)

Marcus, G. (1998) *Ethnography through Thick and Thin*, Princeton, NJ: Princeton University Press.

Chapter 5

Castleton, G., Sanguinetti, G. and Falk, I. (2001) 'Wanted: a new adult literacy policy for Australia', *Literacy and Numeracy Studies* 11 (1): 3–21.

Clanchy, M. (1979) *From Memory to Written Record: England 1066–1377*, London: Edward Arnold.

Gardener, S. (1999–2000) 'Student writing in the 70's and 80's: What we did, why, what happened', *RaPAL Bulletin* 40: 8–12.

Gurnah, A. (2000) 'Languages and literacies for autonomy', in M. Martin-Jones and K. Jones (eds) *Multilingual Literacies*, Amsterdam: John Benjamins.

Hamilton, M. (1996) 'Adult literacy and basic education', in R. Fieldhouse (ed.) *A History of Modern British Adult Education*, Leicester: NIACE.

Hamilton, M. (1998) 'Keeping alternative visions alive', *RaPAL Bulletin* 36.

Hamilton, M. and Merrifield, J. (2000) 'Adult learning and literacy in the United Kingdom', in J. Comings. B. Gardner and C. Smith (eds) *The Annual Review of Adult Learning and Literacy*, vol. 1, San Francisco: Jossey-Bass.

Mace, J. (ed.) (1995) *Literacy, Language and Community Publishing*, Clevedon: Multilingual Matters.

Mace, J. (2002) *The Give and Take of Writing: Scribes, Literacy and Everyday Life*. Leicester: NIACE.

Morris, C. and Nwenmely, H. (1994) 'The Keyol language and literacy project', in M. Hamilton, D. Barton and R. Ivanič (eds) *Worlds of Literacy*, Clevedon: Multilingual Matters.

Pecket Well College (1994) 'Forging a common language, sharing the power', in M. Hamilton, D. Barton and R. Ivanič (eds) *Worlds of Literacy*, Clevedon: Multilingual Matters.

Pitt, K. (2004) *The Right to Read Campaign*, unpublished research paper for ESRC Changing Faces Project, Lancaster: Lancaster University.

Schwab, I. (1994) 'Literacy, language variety and identity', in M. Hamilton, D. Barton and R. Ivanič (eds) *Worlds of Literacy*, Clevedon: Multilingual Matters.

Searle, J. (1999) *Discourses of Literacy*, Queensland: Language Australia.

Sticht, T.G. (2002) 'The rise of the adult education and literacy system in the United States: 1600–2000', in J. Comings, B. Gardner and C. Smith (eds) *The Annual Review of Adult Learning and Literacy*, San Francisco: Jossey-Bass.

Street, B.V. (1997) *Adult Literacy in the United Kingdom: A History of Research and Practice*, RaPAL.

Vincent, D. (2000) *The Rise of Mass Literacy: Reading and Writing in Modern Europe*, Oxford: Polity Press.

Withnall, A. (1994) 'Literacy on the agenda: the origins of the adult literacy campaign in the United Kingdom', *Studies in the Education of Adults* 26 (1): 67–85.

Chapter 6

Ade-ojo, G.O. (2004) 'The new national ESOL curriculum: is it determined by convention?', *RaPAL Bulletin*, 53: 21–28.

Crowther, J., Hamilton, M. and Tett, L. (2001) (eds) *Powerful Literacies*, Leicester: NIACE.

DfEE (2001a) *Skills for Life: The National Strategy for Improving Adult Literacy and Numeracy Skills*. Executive summary, Nottingham: DfEE Publications.

DfES (2002a) *Delivering Skills for Life*, Nottingham: DfES Publications.

DfES (2003a) Skills for Life, *Annual Review 2002–2003*, Nottingham: DfES Publications.

Hamilton, M. (1998) 'Keeping alternative visions alive', *RaPAL Bulletin*, 36.

Hamilton, M. and Merrifield, J. (2000) 'Adult learning and literacy in the United Kingdom', in J. Comings, B. Gardner and C. Smith (eds) *The Annual Review of Adult Learning and Literacy*, vol. 1, San Francisco: Jossey-Bass.

Lavender, P., Derrick, J. and Brooks, B. (2004) *'Testing, testing . . .': Assessment in Adult Literacy, Language and Numeracy*, Leicester: NIACE.

OECD (1995) *Literacy, Economy and Society: Results of the First International Literacy Survey*, Paris: CEDI.

OECD (2000) *Literacy in the Information Age*. Paris: OECD.

OECD/CERI (1997) *Education Policy Analysis*. Paris: OECD.

OECD/Human Resources Development Canada (1997) *Literacy Skills for the Knowledge Society. Further Results from the International Adult Literacy Survey*, Paris: OECD.

Chapter 7

Black, S. (2004) 'Whose economic wellbeing? A challenge to dominant discourses on the relationship between literacy/numeracy skills and (un)employment', *Literacy and Numeracy Studies* 13 (1): 7–17.

Bynner, J. and Parsons, S. (1997) *It Doesn't Get Any Better: The Impact of Poor Basic Skills on the Lives of 37-year-olds*. London: Basic Skills Agency.

DfEE (2001b) *Skills for Life: The National Strategy for Improving Adult Literacy and Numeracy Skills*. Nottingham: DfEE Publications.

DfES (2002) *Skills for Life. The National Strategy for Improving Adult Literacy and Numeracy Skills: The First Year*. 2001–02, Nottingham: DfES Publications.

DfES (2004) *Skills for Life, Annual Review 2003–2004*, Nottingham: DfES Publications.

Fairclough, N. (2003) *Analysing Discourse. Text Analysis for Social Research*, London: Routledge.

Gowen, S. (1992) *The Politics of Workplace Literacy: a Case Study*, New York: Teachers College Press.

Hamilton, M. and Barton, D. (2000) 'The International Literacy Survey: what does it measure?' *International Review of Education* 46 (5): 377–389.

Hull, G. (1993) '"Hearing other voices": a critical assessment of popular views on literacy and work', *Harvard Educational Review* 63 (1): 20–49.

OECD/Stats Canada (1995) *Literacy, Economy and Society: Results of the First International Adult Literacy Survey*, Paris: OECD.

OECD (2000) *Literacy in the Information Age*, Paris: OECD.

Wymer, K. (1998) 'Bilston Community College's policy on adult literacy, basic skills and employment', in Bilston Community College (ed.) *Basic Skills and Further Education*, Bilston: Bilston Community College (in association with Education Now Publishing, Derby).

Chapter 8

Auerbach, E. (1999) 'Teacher, tell me what to do' in I. Shor and C. Pars (eds) *Critical Literacy in Action*, Portsmouth: Boynton/Cook.

Barton, D. (1994) *Literacy – The Ecology of Written Language*, London: Blackwell.

Barton, D. and Hamilton, M. (1998) *Local Literacies*, London: Routledge.

Castleton, G. (2001) 'The role of literacy in people's lives: a case study of its use amongst the homeless in Australia', in J. Crowther, M. Hamilton and L. Tett (eds) *Powerful Literacies*, Leicester: NIACE.

Chouliaraki, L. and Fairclough, N. (1999) *Discourse in Late Modernity*, Cambridge: CUP.

Clark, R. and Ivanič, R. (1998) 'Critical discourse analysis and educational change', in L. van Lier and D. Corson (eds) *The Encyclopedia of Language and Education, Volume 6: Knowledge About Language*, Dordrecht: Kluwer.

CLPN Community Literacy Project Nepal, http://www.clpn.org.

Crowther, J. and Tett, L. (2001) 'Democracy as a way of life: literacy for citizenship', in J. Crowther, M. Hamilton and L. Tett (eds) *Powerful Literacies*, Leicester: NIACE, pp. 108–121.

Degener, S.C. (2001) 'Making sense of critical pedagogy in adult literacy education', in J. Comings, B. Gardner and C. Smith (eds) *The Annual Review of Adult Learning and Literacy*, vol. 2, San Francisco: Jossey-Bass.

Ewing, G. (2003) 'The New Literacy Studies: a point of contact between literacy research and literacy work', *Literacies* (1): 15–21.

Fairclough, N. (1992) *Critical Language Awareness*, London: Longman.

Fairclough, N. (1995) *Critical Discourse Analysis*, London: Longman.

Fairclough, N. (2003) *Analysing Discourse. Textual Analysis for Social Research*. London: Routledge.

Gee, J.P. (1996) *Social Linguistics and Literacies*, 2nd edn, London: Taylor & Francis.

Gee, J.P. (2004) *Situated Language and Learning*, London: Routledge.

Hamilton, M. (1996) 'Adult literacy and basic education', in R. Fieldhouse (ed.) *A History of Modern British Adult Education*, Leicester: NIACE.

Hamilton, M. (1999) 'Ethnography for classrooms: constructing a reflective curriculum for literacy', *Pedagogy, Culture and Society* 7 (3): 429–444.

Hamilton, M. (2000) 'Sustainable literacies and the ecology of lifelong learning', Supporting Lifelong Learning Colloquium, London, July 2000. Available: http://www.open.ac.uk/lifelong-learning/papers/index.html (accessed 10.9.04).

Hamilton, M. and Merrifield, J. (2000) 'Adult learning and literacy in the United Kingdom', in J. Comings, B. Gardner and C. Smith (eds) *The Annual Review of Adult Learning and Literacy*, vol. 1, San Francisco: Jossey-Bass.

Hull, G. and Schultz, K. (2002) 'Connecting schools with out-of-school worlds', in G. Hull and K. Schultz (eds) *School's Out!* New York: Teachers College Press.

Ivanič, R. (1990) 'Critical language awareness in action', in R. Carter (ed.) *Knowledge about Language and the Curriculum: The LINC Reader*, London: Hodder & Stoughton.

Janks, H. and Ivanič, R. (1992) 'Critical language awareness and emancipatory discourse', in N. Fairclough (ed.) *Critical Language Awareness*. London: Longman.

Jessop, M., Lawrence, G. and Pitt, K. (1998) 'Two workshops on critical literary practice', *RaPAL Bulletin* 35: 13–16.

Kulick, D. and Stroud, C. (1993) 'Conceptions and uses of literacy in a Papua New Guinean village', in B.V. Street (ed.) *Cross-cultural Approaches to Literacy*, Cambridge: CUP.

Millican, J. (2004) '"I will stay here until I die": a critical analysis of the Muthande Literacy Programme', in A. Robinson-Pant (ed.) *Women, Literacy and Development*, London: Routledge.

Rogers, A., Maddox, B., Millican, J., Newell-Jones, K., Papen, U. and Robinson-Pant, A. (1999) *Re-defining Post-literacy in a Changing World*, London: Department for International Development, Education Research, Serial No. 29.

Shore, S. (2003) 'What's whiteness got to do with it?' *Literacies* 2: 19–25.

Smith, D. (1990) *Texts, Facts and Femininity*, London: Routledge.

Street, B.V. (1993) 'Introduction: the new literacy studies', in B.V. Street (ed.) *Cross-Cultural Approaches to Literacy*. Cambridge: CUP.

Street, B.V. (with Street, J.) (1995) 'The schooling of literacy', in B.V. Street, *Social Literacies: Critical Approaches to Literacy in Development, Ethnography and Education*, London and New York: Longman.

Street, B.V. (1997) 'The implications of the "New Literacy Studies" for literacy education', *English in Education* 31 (3): 45–59.

Wodak, R. and Meyer, M. (ed.) (2001) *Methods of Critical Discourse Analysis*, London: Sage.

Conclusions

Crowther, J., Hamilton M. and Tett, L. (2001) 'Powerful literacies: an introduction', in J. Crowther, M. Hamilton and L.Tett (eds) *Powerful Literacies*, Leicester: NIACE.

Gee, J., Hull, G. and Lanksheer, C. (1996) *The New Work Order: Behind the Language of the New Capitalism*, London: Allen & Unwin.

Hamilton, M. and Merrifield, J. (2000) 'Adult learning and literacy in the United Kingdom', in J. Comings, B. Garner and C. Smith (eds) *The Annual Review of Adult Learning and Literacy*, vol. 1, San Francisco: Jossey-Bass.

Martin, I. and Rahman, H. (2001) 'The politics of really useful literacy: six lessons from Bangladesh, in J. Crowther, M. Hamilton and L. Tett (eds) *Powerful Literacies*, Leicester: NIACE.

McCabe, C. (1998) ' A response to Brian Street', *English in Education* 32 (1): 26–28.

Merchant, G. (2001) 'Teenagers in cyberspace – an investigation of language use and language change in internet chatrooms', *Journal of Research in Reading* 24 (3): 293–306.

Index